BULLIES AND BYSTANDERS

BULLIES AND BYSTANDERS

Understanding and Challenging Bullying in Churches and Christian Groups

EDITED BY JANET FIFE AND ANNE LEE

DARTON · LONGMAN + TODD

INTELLIGENT ◆ INSPIRATIONAL ◆ INCLUSIVE
SPIRITUAL BOOKS

First published in 2026 by
Darton, Longman and Todd Ltd
Unit 1, The Exchange
6 Scarbrook Road
Croydon CR0 1UH
editorial@darton-longman-todd.co.uk

This product conforms to the requirements of the European Union's
General Product Safety Regulations (GPSR).
EU Authorised Representative for GPSR:
Easy Access System Europe –
Mustamäe tee 50, 10621 Tallinn, Estonia
gpsr.requests@easproject.com

ISBN: 978-1-915412-40-9

Printed and bound in Great Britain by Bell & Bain, Glasgow.

Contents

Foreword   11
by ROWAN WILLIAMS

Preface   15

Our Authors   19

1 **Introduction**   25
   ANNE LEE

2 **What is Bullying?**   35
   ANNE LEE

3 **Trouble at St Chad's**   45
   RUTH CARTER

4 **Hope, Exile and Renewal:**   51
   A Church of England Curate's Story
   JAMES MERTON

5 **A Question of Trust**   63
   JAMES GIBSON

6 **Faith, Hope and Disillusionment**   71
   EVE FOSTER

7   **Bullied into Silence**   79
    ANNE SAMUELS

8   **'My Life Will Never Be the Same':**   87
    The Psychodynamics of Workplace
    Bullying and the Inner World of the Bully
    FIONA GARDNER

9   **The Traumatic Impact of Bullying**   95
    RHONA KNIGHT

10 **Silencing and Retraumatising**   103
    REBECCA PARNABY-ROOKE

11 **Barriers to Addressing Bullying in**   111
    Congregational Settings
    LORRAINE TURNER

12 **Why Do People Find it Difficult to**   119
    Grasp the Nettle of Bullying?
    ANNE LEE

13 **Bullying, Power and Hierarchy**   127
    JOY ALLAN

14 **Bullying and its Enablers**   135
    DEIRDRE GOOD

15 **The Post Office at Prayer**   143
    MARTYN PERCY

16 **The Empire Strikes Back: The**   151
    Intersection of Race, Sexuality and
    Ministry as it Relates to Bullying
    AUGUSTINE TANNER-IHM

17 **Shunning as a Method of Control in Authoritarian Churches** 157
STEPHEN PARSONS

18 **Cyber Bullying** 165
CLIVE BILLENNESS

19 **Bullying in Religious Settings: The Impact on Faith** 173
JONATHAN ABERNETHY-BARKLEY

20 **Watching Blood Flow Under the Door** 179
ALISON KENNEDY

21 **Bullying and Harassment in the Church of England: Legal Remedies** 189
Richard Scorer and Cecilia Davies

22 **What Are the Churches Doing About Bullying?** 199
ANNE LEE

23 **What I've Learned from Bullies** 211
JANET FIFE

Bibliography 219

Foreword

We often see reminders in public places that 'not every disability is visible'. Something of the same might be said about bullying. It seems still to be possible for institutions to deny that there is a problem in their cultures and habits, even as the record builds up of lives damaged and undermined by behaviours that are not properly named or challenged. The Christian churches are still painfully slow in acknowledging this human cost; anyone, like myself, who has been involved in the administration of the Church should be asking, 'What have I missed? What have I implicitly colluded with?' That is why this book is uncomfortable reading for me, and will be so for others.

The problem exists at several levels, of course. We are slowly waking up to how we can more effectively recognise the more overt signs of bullying habits and cultures, the kinds of behaviour that encode a deep-seated lack of patient attention to others – to the 'invisible' vulnerabilities they carry and to the reactions that they feel, and the long-term effects of such reactions in their work and their sense of self. Sometimes people have a salutary shock as they realise just what the impact of their behaviour can be. I can remember from many years ago a parish meeting where a priest, at the end of his tether with the congregation's collective aggressiveness, told them point-blank how he and his wife were feeling; people's pained surprise and embarrassment were very plain. A mirror had been held up to them, and it began to break something of a deadlock.

But sometimes we are talking about the dark excitement of cruelty, people who know quite well how their words and actions will impact on others, and who know where the tender spots are. It's a classic bullying style; ironically, it depends on a kind of perverse psychological insight, an instinct for what will hurt and demean. It can be rationalised in all sorts of ways, but it displays a deep problem that needs not only naming but also engaging and (ideally) healing. So many people will have internalised models of authority that work like this and are drawn to contexts and positions where they can give full rein to ways of acting and relating that reinforce their sense of power. Power, after all, is seldom if ever just a matter of being able to get people to do what you want; it is also to do with the satisfaction of knowing how to make them *feel*.

And then – still more uncomfortably – there is what seems to be an increasingly pervasive issue these days. We are very much invested in procedures that allow us to measure progress, success, risk, and so on. Training models for ministry are dominated by reporting systems more rigorous than they used to be. Safeguarding systems and disciplinary processes are complex and detailed (and slow-moving). The monitoring of performance in so many areas can appear relentless. (And in all these respects, the Church's ministry is experiencing much the same as most other professions.)

We all know why. We have a history of – at best – bland carelessness about these things, and – at worst – a kind of collective laziness and inattention to the scale of human cost involved in corrupt and abusive behaviours. No one could or should defend any of this history. But we still need a bit more literacy about how some of these things can be handled. We need to notice the risks of creating a climate of profound anxiety and disempowerment for both clergy and laity. Training programmes for both can be experienced as perfunctory and 'box-ticking', inadequately explained and grounded. In the safeguarding world, both complainants and accused can be heard expressing bewilderment or anger; they will sometimes be taken aback at what they feel as a sidelining of 'natural justice' and an opaque and unchallengeable process of decision-making, in which care for individuals is not always much in evidence. As institutions, the Churches have not yet quite learned how to consolidate the need for proper accountability without giving way to the temptations of a defensive and sometimes artificial build-up of protocols to show that all righteousness has been fulfilled – in ways that can leave people feeling lost, abandoned, manipulated and stigmatised. Feeling bullied, in fact.

In all these varieties and levels of behaviour experienced as bullying, what we see in the Church is a widespread failure to think through what is actually involved in being the Body of Christ. We are failing to let ourselves be formed by the Spirit – that is, to be formed into persons who are always aware of our indebtedness to one another for the daily renewal of the Good News and our obligation to share that Good News. One basic question for any believer is 'How do my words and acts convey the Gospel to the person I am dealing with? How can I both show and stimulate thankfulness?'

Cultures of bullying and manipulation are the polar opposite to all this. Which is why ultimately the problem needs cultural change, not *only* better regulation. But without a clarity of diagnosis and a realistic, robust means of identifying where things are wrong, we shall not arrive at such cultural transformation. The root issues are finally to do with how we believe authority is exercised and received. Authority in the Church is not the power to achieve goals but the freedom to heal and liberate: that is how the authority of Jesus in the gospels is insistently, unmistakably presented to us. As such it is an authority shared with every believer, not simply exercised by individuals (ordained or not) to bring others into line. What are we doing as Churches to deepen formation in that kind of authority, an authority vindicated by its power to heal? That is surely one of the deepest and hardest questions that this timely book leaves us with.

Rowan Williams
Cardiff, Lent 2026

Preface

It is a sad fact that wherever two or three people are gathered together, there is a possibility that at least one of them may bully another. Churches, despite our high ideals, are no exception. Janet comes from a family with six clergy, working in different denominations or organisations; Anne is a lay woman in the Church of England. We have had more than ample opportunity to observe, and sometimes painfully experience, bullying among Christians in a number of contexts. Some of the issues regarding bullies and their targets are the same everywhere but other aspects are particular to Christian organisations, their structures, and their ideology. We saw a need to address these issues with a focus on churches and religious organisations mainly (but not exclusively) in the UK.

Our contributors come from a variety of backgrounds and denominations and write from different points of view. Their views are their own, and may differ at times from those of the editors, but each contribution is valuable and each voice deserves to be heard. We are privileged that each of the contributors has taken the trouble to write for us, and we thank them for their expertise, courage, and honesty.

Chapters One and Two provide background to the subject of bullying, and a little general information on the Christian scene in the UK. They are followed by first-person accounts from people who have been targeted by bullies. As you read them, look out for the bystanders and enablers who may be present but not identified as such. These accounts will have been difficult and painful to write; for some it has been even more painful that, for legal reasons, they have had to use a pseudonym. Bullies seek to erase our identity and compromise our wholeness as a child of God; having to be anonymous compounds that erasure. We are grateful to our contributors for having told their stories, despite the cost, with a view to helping others.

After the personal accounts there are chapters dealing with specialist aspects, written by people with professional or academic expertise. Some, such as the chapter on bullying and harassment in the Church of England, will have wider applications than their particular focus might suggest. And it's worth remembering that those writing personal accounts may also have professional expertise, and those writing analytically may have personal experience. There is considerable crossover.

The book concludes with a note of hope: bullies do not need to have the last word, and God can work in and through our situations and suffering to bring us new life. The Spirit of the Lord still works 'to bring good news to the poor, release to the captives, recovery of sight to the blind, and to let the oppressed go free' (Luke 4:18).

We would like to thank David Moloney of Darton, Longman and Todd, who has encouraged us along the way, and been patient when ill health and bereavements delayed the project for several years. The contributors who had already completed their chapters also showed remarkable patience with long delays. Many others helped this book come to fruition, including Anne's daughter Kate (1971-2023), also a psychologist, who worked with Anne as her research assistant and made many very significant contributions to her research. Other friends were important allies; in particular, Gill Brentford who started Anne on the path she has taken.

A final note: for clarity, we have used a capital 'C' for denominations such as the Church of England and the Roman Catholic Church and for the Church worldwide. When individual and local churches are meant, 'church' is spelled with a small 'c'.

All Bible quotations are taken from the New Revised Standard Version unless otherwise specified.

It is our hope that this book will contribute to a better understanding of bullying, and a greater will to tackle it.

Our Authors

EDITORS

Anne Lee is a social psychologist. She has taught undergraduates and postgraduates in the University of Oxford for thirty years. Her research area is workplace bullying, particularly in churches and other religious groups. She has written extensively and spoken internationally on bullying in churches.

Janet Fife is a retired Anglican priest and writer. She has a research degree in the pastoral care of sexual abuse survivors and has campaigned for some years on issues of abuse. Previous books include *To Be Honest* and *Letters to a Broken Church* (co-editor).

CONTRIBUTORS

Revd Dr Jonathan Abernethy-Barkley is a minister; a lecturer at Kings College, London, exploring the relevance of faith to childhood sexual abuse; and a researcher at the University of Aberdeen working on the 'Race and Class in UK Religious Studies and Theology' project. He is from Northern Ireland and grew up during the Troubles.

Dr Joy Allan is a theologian whose expertise lies in pastoral care, particularly in the fields of mental health, theology, and abuse. Following her PhD she worked for a few years as a lecturer in Practical Theology. She now works for the *Difference* course, which is a reconciliation resource. She believes good relationships and the ways we use and understand power are the key theological and pastoral issues of our time.

Clive Billenness. After retiring as a Senior Research Fellow specialising in IT Project Management, Clive became a member of the General Synod of the Church of England. Until his untimely death, he campaigned tirelessly alongside other colleagues to fight the injustice met by victims and survivors of many forms of abuse which occurred within church environments. His documentary *Is There a Psychopath in My Parish?* Has been influential. https://www.youtube.com/watchv=UpJCgb5EY2s

'**Ruth Carter**' is a pseudonym.

'**Eve Foster**' says she is 'a Christian peace campaigner, lesbian activist, motivational speaker – and a nuisance!' She is a veteran of the Greenham Common protests against nuclear weapons. 'Eve Foster' is a pseudonym.

Cecilia (Nikki) Davies is a solicitor with expertise in bullying cases.

Fiona Gardner previously worked as a psychoanalytic psychotherapist, and as a Church of England diocesan safeguarding advisor. She is now a spiritual director and a writer. Her recent publications include: *Taking Heart; Sex, Power, Control: Responding to abuse in the institutional church* and *Night Sea Journeying: soul recovery from childhood trauma.*

'**James Gibson**' has been a member of several Roman Catholic and ecumenical religious communities. He is a former therapist and journalist, and has run a Scottish charity for people living with HIV/Aids. He is now retired and lives in Edinburgh. 'James Gibson' is a pseudonym.

Dr Deirdre Good was born in Kenya, and grew up in the UK. She is a New Testament scholar who has held senior academic posts in several US seminaries and universities. She is the author of several books including *Jesus the Meek King*; *Mariam the Magdalen and the Mother*; *Jesus' Family Values*; *A Fortress Introduction: Studying the New Testament* (with Bruce Chilton); *Courage Beyond Fear;* and *Borderlands of Theological Education* (with Josh Davis).

Revd Alison Kennedy served as a parish priest in and around London prior to ministering in a dual role at Chelmsford Cathedral and St Mellitus College. Before ordination, Alison trained, practised, and taught as a music therapist with a particular focus on mental health. She is currently the Cambridge campus chaplain at Anglia Ruskin University and has a particular interest in trauma.

Revd Dr Rhona Knight is a retired GP currently researching trauma in curacy in the Church of England. She is a spiritual director, pastoral supervisor, and a member of the College of Chaplains at Launde Abbey.

'**Revd James Merton**' is a priest in the Church of England. He writes and speaks on equity and inclusion, ethics, chaplaincy, and liberation theology. 'James Merton' is a pseudonym.

Rebecca Parnaby-Rooke is a writer and activist who facilitates the online community The Ordinary Office. A trained music therapist now living with long COVID, Rebecca has previously led musical worship in a variety of churches and is interested in the intersections of music, safeguarding, and disability.

Revd Stephen Parsons is a retired Anglican priest who has a longstanding interest in issues of power within religious institutions. He is a member of the International Cultic Studies Association and the editor of *Surviving Church,* a blog which discusses issues of power, bullying, and abuse within church settings. Stephen is the author of *Ungodly Fear: Fundamentalist Christianity and the Abuse of Power.*

Revd Prof. Martyn Percy is an Anglican priest and Provost-Theologian of Ming Hua College, Hong Kong; Prof. Of Religion and Culture, University of Saint Joseph, Macao; Senior Research Associate, James Hutton Institute, Aberdeen; Research Professor, Theologische Fakultät, Universität Bern; and Canon Theologian, Convocation of Episcopal Churches in Europe. He has written a number of books.

'**Anne Samuels'** is a pseudonym.

Richard Scorer is a solicitor and Head of Abuse Law at Slater and Gordon Lawyers. He acts for victims and survivors of abuse, particularly abuse in religious settings.

Revd Dr Augustine Tanner-Ihm is a Black American minister, industrial psychologist, creative, and activist.

Revd Dr Lorraine Turner has served in Church of England parish ministry for 20 years. Alongside this, she has used her research to offer Continuing Ministerial Development, which helps clergy begin to talk about bullying. She has recently become Transition Priest for the Kerry Group of Churches in the Diocese of St Asaph, Church in Wales.

Lord Rowan Williams of Oystermouth was Archbishop of Canterbury between 2002 and 2012. Prior to that he was Archbishop of Wales for three years, and Bishop of Monmouth for eleven years. He is acknowledged internationally as an outstanding theologian, writer and teacher, and has written a number of bestselling books on faith and thought.

1

Introduction

ANNE LEE

Bullying is a topical issue. For many years we have been aware of the problems in schools; high profile cases of children ending their own lives because they have been bullied have hit the headlines all too frequently. Beneath these personal tragedies lie considerable physical, emotional, and spiritual distress caused by bullying; by the inappropriate behaviour of one or more human beings towards another.

A high proportion of workplace bullies are in the caring professions, including the Church. Bullying occurs in a variety of religious contexts. Lay people, church officers, church workers, and clergy can behave abusively to other lay or ordained people. Herein lies the Church's dilemma. Because lay and ordained members aspire to high standards of behaviour, it is often very difficult to believe that other church members fail in reaching these standards, especially as bullying often happens in private.

In the following chapters of this book, you will read heart-breaking stories of people being targeted by a perpetrator of bullying; either because the perpetrator clearly had a problem themselves and the target was in the wrong place at the wrong time, or because of the target's gender, sexual orientation, or race. You will read of the lack of support from those who could reasonably have been expected to be in a position to support a target of bullying, especially those in a senior position in the Church. How did the bullying manifest itself? By the inappropriate use of social media, by exclusion, by having lies told about the target – amongst other unacceptable bullying behaviours. Another chapter will talk about bullying behaviours and possible ways of dealing with them, at greater length.

Historical background in the UK

Bullying in the workplace was first brought to prominence in the UK through a 1990 radio programme titled 'An abuse of power'. The resulting postbag was the largest the BBC had ever received and a follow-up programme, 'Whose fault is it anyway?', was aired in 1991. In 1994 the MSF Union organised a conference on 'Bullying at Work'; in 1996 an Institute of Personnel Development survey of 1,000 workers found that one in eight felt they had been bullied during the previous five years. That bullying was commonplace in their organisation was felt by 50 per cent. ACAS (the Advisory, Conciliation, and Arbitration Service) has evolved from the government's voluntary conciliation and arbitration service set up after the Conciliation Act was passed in 1896. It became an independent statutory body via the Employment Protection Act 1975 and has recently celebrated its fiftieth anniversary. Since 2014, before anyone can lodge an employment tribunal claim, they must notify ACAS of their intention to claim so that ACAS can offer the opportunity to resolve the problems using early conciliation. In the ACAS report *Workplace Trends of 2016*, they say:

> [workplace bullying] is usually understood as an extreme form of unwanted behaviour, but the steady demand for advice from the ACAS Helpline on this

topic – around 20,000 calls a year – indicates that it's a significant and persistent problem.[1]

In November 2015, ACAS had produced a policy discussion paper in which they say:

> Workplace bullying is a serious problem in Britain's workplaces. It is a source of considerable individual suffering and weakens the performance of organisations. Yet, despite a growing awareness of the negative outcomes associated with bullying, and of the significant wider costs to society and the economy, its complexity continues to pose a challenge for those seeking to prevent and manage such behaviours in the workplace. It is also clear that in many workplaces, bullying is not taken seriously enough.[2]

Legal challenges

In the UK there is no legal definition of bullying. A Dignity at Work bill, aimed specifically at the prevention of bullying in the workplace and the provision of effective remedies for the targets of bullying, was steered through Parliament by Lord Monkswell between November 1996 and February 1997. However, it failed to reach the statute books owing to lack of parliamentary time before the General Election in May 1997. An attempt by Baroness Ann Gibson in 2001 to revive it for a second reading also failed. However, the consequent media publicity raised awareness of workplace bullying in the UK and the phrase 'dignity at work' has become embedded within the wider industrial relations debate. Another bill had its first reading in the House of Commons in July 2023, but was, again, out of time because of the general election in 2024. It has had a second reading in the House of Commons in

2025, sponsored by Rachael Maskell MP. The definition of bullying provided by ACAS 2025 is frequently used:

> Bullying can be described as unwanted behaviour from a person or group that is either:
>
> 1. offensive, intimidating, malicious or insulting
> 2. an abuse or misuse of power that undermines, humiliates, or causes physical or emotional harm to someone
>
> Bullying might:
>
> 1. be a regular pattern of behaviour or a one-off incident
> 2. happen face-to-face, on social media, in emails or calls
> 3. happen at work or in other work-related situations
> 4. not always be obvious or noticed by others.

Harassment, however, is clearly defined under the 2010 Equality Act which requires equal treatment in access to employment as well as private and public services, regardless of the nine protected characteristics of age, disability, gender reassignment, marriage and civil partnership, pregnancy and maternity, race, religion or belief, sex, and sexual orientation. The Equality Act prohibits:

> Unwanted conduct related to a relevant protected characteristic, which has the purpose or effect of violating an individual's dignity or creating an intimidating, hostile, degrading, humiliating or offensive environment for that individual.

The government went on to define what this might mean for churches:

> In the case of Ministers of Religion and other jobs which exist to promote and represent religion, the Bill recognises that a church may need to impose requirements regarding sexual orientation, sex, marriage and civil partnership or gender reassignment if it is necessary to comply with its teachings or the strongly held beliefs of followers. However, it would not be right to permit such requirements across all jobs within organised religions, such as administrators and accountants, and the Equality Bill makes this clear.

Unfortunately harassment is only outlawed in relation to the nine protected characteristics of the 2010 Equality Act.

The Church as a workplace

Churches are complex organisations. In the United Kingdom, church workers fall into three categories:

- Office Holders
- Employees
- Volunteers.

There are many complexities in the employment status of clergy. In most denominations they are classified, by case law and the Churches, as office holders because a direct contract between the clergy and their employer cannot be identified. They rarely have recourse to employment law. However, not all clergy are office holders; some, including some school or healthcare chaplains, have a contract of employment. In the Church of England, some clergy are employed by their Parochial Church Council (PCC) as extra clergy when the individual parish feels there is the need and is able to afford it. Their stipends are paid by the parish.

Church of England clergy who hold office under common tenure are entitled to a written statement of particulars which sets out the rights and obligations of office holders conferred by the Ecclesiastical Terms of Service Measure and Regulations. This is supported by their diocesan *Common Tenure Guide*, which provides additional and more detailed information. The chapter by Richard Scorer and Cecilia Davies gives more information about the employment status of clergy and legal recourse for those who are bullied.

Volunteers do not receive payment for the activity or work they do. In the last few years several charities with large numbers of volunteers 'working' for them have written agreements setting out what the volunteer may and may not do. However, at least in the UK, churches very rarely have any such agreement in place. The majority of church members and church attenders can be described as volunteers. Some clergy are volunteers, though they are also normally classed as office holders. According to the UK census, church attendance is classified as a leisure activity.

Governance

The structure of the different denominations is all-important, as the paragraphs below demonstrate. This section is not intended to be exhaustive, but demonstrates how the governance of churches in the UK varies according to denomination. The form of governance is vital when looking at dealing with issues such as bullying and harassment, or other types of abuse. One size definitely does not fit all. There are of course, other religious groups, but the following demonstrates the legal difficulties many churches have when dealing with abuse of any sort.

- *Roman Catholic Church.* The Catholic Council of Bishops for England and Wales is the decision-making body of the Catholic Church. Their decisions must be implemented in every Catholic parish in England and Wales.

- *Church of England.* Each of the 43 dioceses of the Church of England is autonomous. Neither the national Church nor the archbishops are able to require any diocese to do, or not do, anything. There are 42 dioceses covering the geographical area of England. A 43rd diocese is even more complex: the Diocese in Europe covers more than 40 countries and 83 legal jurisdictions. The Scottish Episcopal Church and the Church in Wales are also Anglican churches and members of the Anglican Communion, but are not part of the Church of England.

- *Methodist Church.* The Methodist Church is still organised in the methodical way introduced by its founder, John Wesley, and still uses many of the structures he devised. Decisions made by the annual Methodist Conference must be accepted by all Methodist churches. Methodist Conference is supported by a Connexional Council which meets several times a year. There are 23 geographical districts across England, Scotland, Wales, the Isle of Man and the Channel Islands. Districts are made up of groupings of local churches called circuits. Methodist ministers are appointed to circuits; (lay) local preachers have nationally recognised accreditation and lead worship in the circuit in which they are members.

- *Baptist Church.* Baptist churches in the United Kingdom are governed by a congregational system. Each local church is self-governing and autonomous, with members of the church making key decisions through church meetings. They may belong to the national Baptist Union of Great Britain (BUGB) for support, resources, and shared mission, and there are regional associations.

Besides these main denominations there are many smaller Churches (including around half a dozen Pentecostal and several breakaway Catholic and Anglican Churches), each with its own structure and governance. Associations of independent churches, such as the Evangelical Alliance and the Fellowship of Independent Evangelical Churches, provide shared resources and fellowship without too much control. There are a plethora of other Christian organisations: mission societies, campaign organisations, religious communities, schools and colleges, publishers, retreat houses, and so on. Most are charities. Sadly, bullying can occur in every denomination and in every Christian organisation and workplace.

Bullying can be both overt and covert. In churches it is more likely to be covert, which means that there are often no other people to witness the bullying. Or, the bullying may seem to an onlooker to be so trivial that no intervention is necessary. Unfortunately a long succession of apparently trivial bullying behaviours may trigger what seems to be an unreasonable response from the person to whom they are directed, the target, for example in a church Council meeting, at a church coffee morning or other event.

Bystanders

A bystander is an observer of an event or situation. He or she is an onlooker of a situation, who often chooses not to intervene. However, there is often no reason why a bystander should remain passive. They do not need to remain on the sidelines. Bystanders are important people who can testify to the bullying behaviour as they have witnessed it; they can also intervene and try to stop it. Watching and ignoring a bullying situation is not a passive event. It effectively says to the perpetrator that they can carry on with their bullying behaviour because nobody is going to do anything about it. At this point a bystander becomes an enabler of bullying. A challenge for churches and parachurch organisations is to turn a passive bystander into a responsible, active one. Somebody who is able to recognise the behaviour they are seeing or hearing as bullying behaviour, who is able to challenge it and offer support to the target; somebody who is able to interrupt the scenario and de-escalate the situation; somebody who is able to seek help from others and act to support the target and make sure the perpetrator receives appropriate sanctions.

Enablers

Enablers are people who have either seen the bullying which is happening and ignored it or they can be people who have been told about the bullying and decided to do nothing. In these situations the perpetrator is effectively 'given permission' to continue their bullying behaviours. Enablers are often the people to whom the bullying has been reported. In churches, enablers are frequently members of the senior staff to whom a target has gone both for support, but also action. Interpreting the behaviour as 'trivial', minimising it or describing it, for example, as a 'personality clash' simply encourages the perpetrator to continue their behaviour. The person making that interpretation has become an enabler of bullying.

---

1   *Workplace Trends of 2016* (ACAS), p. 12.

2   Evesson, Justine, Oxenbridge, Sarah, and Taylor, David, *Seeking Better Solutions: tackling bullying and ill-treatment in Britain's workplaces* (ACAS, 2015), p. 1. https://www.acas.org.uk/research-and-commentary/seeking-better-solutions-tackling-bullying-and-ill-treatment/paper

2

What is Bullying?

ANNE LEE

Bullying is abuse. It can be a subtle form of abuse that is difficult to identify. Constant criticism, verbal abuse, unrealistic expectations and manipulation are all examples of bullying behaviours, but it is the sustained nature of the abuse, and the context in which it happens, that turns seemingly minor or apparently trivial incidents into seriously damaging abuse.

Bullying in the Church

> The Church is required by God to foster relationships of the utmost integrity, truthfulness and trustworthiness. Abuse, harassment and bullying will not be tolerated within the Church of England. All complaints of abuse, harassment and bullying are to be taken seriously and thoroughly investigated.[1]

We see that in 2001 the House of Bishops recognised that 'abuse, harassment and bullying' existed in the Church. Unfortunately it was not until 2008, with the publication of *Dignity at Work,* that there were any suggested policies or procedures to be used, and then only if dioceses accepted and implemented them. Sadly this report became out of date on 1 October 2010 when the Equalities Act (2010) came into force.

Although workplace bullying has been shown to have a high profile within the commercial world, the trades unions, the legal profession, and the academic community, there seems to have been very little attempt within church organisations in the UK to take the issue seriously. Evidence suggests that the problem of bullying within churches and religious organisations is widespread and endemic.[2] In July 2006 international, national, and church media carried articles about the revoking of the license of a priest in the Anglican Diocese of Europe, apparently following bullying by a few powerful members of a congregation. The result was a payout of thousands of pounds' compensation for unfair dismissal.[3] Anglican clergy in the UK rarely have access to legal redress, however, as most are office holders and therefore not legally employed; in 2004 fewer than 13 per cent had contracts of employment.[4] In many cases litigation, were it available, would not be appropriate.

Bullying has seriously damaging effects on the physical and psychological health of targets, their families and friends, and other witnesses or bystanders. It also has detrimental effects on the mission of the Church. Therefore the Church should not ignore bullying behaviour, however difficult it may be to define or understand, or indeed to accept that it happens within our churches and para-church organisations.

Over the last few years there have been a number of allegations of bullying and misconduct in charities, including Christian charities: for example Soul Survivor, UCCF (Universities and Colleges Christian Fellowship), and World Vision.

Bullying behaviours found in churches are frequently covert, including:

- Social exclusion
- Spreading malicious rumours
- Unfair treatment
- Deliberate undermining
- Blocking training opportunities
- Deliberately withholding information
- Gossip
- Removing areas of responsibility without discussion or notice
- Setting out to make someone appear incompetent
- Use of emails, either to the individual or to third parties, to reprimand, insult, or otherwise inform someone of their apparent failings.

One of the problems is that the bullying often starts off in a very small, apparently trivial way. So the target is likely to say, 'Am I being over-sensitive?'; 'The issues seem too trivial to deal with'; 'If I ignore it and do nothing, I'm sure it will go away'; or 'Perhaps they were just trying to be funny'.

> We find it almost impossible to explain how the bullying started because so much of it was very gradual and subtle. We had the misfortune to stumble across two or three people for whom bullying was a way of life. They held positions of leadership within the congregation, leadership which they abused by dominating and controlling everyone around them to the extent of 'seeing off' anyone who refused to comply with their order. It began with vaguely critical comments made (pleasantly enough) at church meetings and after services, which on their own sounded harmless and too trivial to answer, but which subtly began to undermine other people's respect for us and our ministry. No doubt this was backed up

with similar comments behind our backs. Then there were the continual nit-picking criticisms addressed to us privately which began, almost imperceptibly at first, to chip away at our self-confidence. There were threats to withdraw money from the church if I didn't do as I was told, threats to destroy our ministry, and threats to make things very difficult for me. Various attempts were made to discredit my wife and to blame her for the problems. She was excluded from meetings, and spiteful, untrue rumours were circulated about her.[4]

Targets

Bullying vocabulary has made one important change since 1992. People once described as 'victims' are now called 'targets'.

> It is recognised that the target is vulnerable merely by being in the wrong place at the wrong time and infers [sic] no complicity or interactivity in the situation beyond reacting (normally) to the bullying behaviour.[5]

This perception is sometimes difficult for church members and leaders to understand and accept. When 'victim' vocabulary is being used, it is easy to ascribe some of the blame to the 'victim(s)' and to assume their behaviour must in some way be contributing to, if not causing, the bullying they are receiving. This is akin to claiming that rape victims are in some way responsible for their sexual assault.

Bullying can have a profound and damaging effect on an individual whether in childhood or as an adult. As a result of bullying the target may struggle to cope with aspects of their day-to-day life and feel an array of different emotions which can have a seriously negative effect on their mental health and wellbeing. For example:

- Stress
- Anxiety
- Depression or feelings of sadness
- Feelings of worthlessness
- Post-traumatic stress disorder
- Low self-esteem or confidence issues
- Isolation or loneliness
- Trouble sleeping
- Physical illness.

The following are examples of brief comments from targets of bullying:

'I had no help from the bishop of the diocese. When I wrote and asked for help, he ignored me. I was on sick leave for seven months and neither he nor the archdeacon nor anyone else visited me. I was even refused the proper help I should have received from a member of the bishop's team. The Church needs to learn how to treat people properly and pastorally and with real respect for employment law. This law has to apply to clergy of the Church of England and bishops can't just think they are above the law.'

'The bishop has not been useful. At all. His oversight of and care for the parish have been almost non-existent. His handling of the situation appears to have been inept and profoundly unhelpful.'

'It is obvious in this diocese, that as far as the clergy are concerned – if there is trouble ahead – you're on your own.'

'As clergy you are brought up to equate God and the Church and when the Church does something awful to you, you have to do some kind of mental readjustment to try and convince yourself that God is okay and it's the people in the church who have got it wrong. I think I am still going through that.'

'He said I was continually insulting him. So the archdeacon asked him to say how I was insulting him. We then witnessed an hour-long tirade of shouting and screaming with the most extraordinary untrue allegations about me and my wife. Later, the archdeacon trivialised it as a personality clash.'

'The diocese wanted us to have mediation. But being asked to be in the same room as the perpetrator is like being asked to be in the same room as your rapist.'

'I tried and tried to get somebody to listen to me, somebody in the hierarchy. But nobody would listen. This is the first time I have been able to tell my story. Thank you for listening.'

'Bullying is more about destroying people's professional capabilities by nit-picking. It is like the drip, drip of Chinese water torture. We have been to hell and back.'

'Being bullied damages the deepest parts of who you are. It shapes your life; no one should have to deal with the negative effects of bullying.'

Overt bullying such as physical abuse has been reported much less frequently, though two respondents in one study reported:

> '[I] was pushed against the wall of the manse hallway and held there while a taller man, a church elder,

leant forward and shouted loudly into [my] ear. In addition to the fear experienced, there was the physical pain of being held, nausea caused by the fear and the trauma of the unacceptably loud noise [I] was being subjected to. The elder said that he had been compelled by God to come and reprimand [me] and wanted to be sure that [I] had no excuse to claim that the voice of God had not been heard.'[6]

The second respondent reported:

'At the end of the [induction] service, the worship leader reminded me that the previous minister had left due to a breakdown and had died shortly after. I made sympathetic noises and a mental note to visit soon and discuss what might be a feeling of grief. He then whispered to me, 'I killed the last one and I can kill you too.' With that we both proceeded into the hall for the induction tea.'[7]

Bystanders

One of the problems with addressing bullying in churches is that most of the bullying happens in private, so there are no witnesses. However, there will be occasions when other people are witnesses to the bullying behaviour. Because each specific incident may seem 'trivial', especially in the beginning, any bystanders may not even notice it. But if they do, it is really important that they offer support to the target. As the 2008 report *Dignity at Work* says:

[witnesses] may be reluctant to come forward as witnesses, as they too may fear the consequences for themselves. Witnesses should be treated with the same confidentiality as the complainant. Perpetrators of bullying can sometimes manipulate witnesses and people need to be aware of this. Sometimes a witness may seek protection from the bully by not supporting the target or even colluding with the bully. (p. 9)

Cyberbullying (bullying using the internet, emails, social media), on the other hand, is visible on whatever internet platform is being used, so that the comments are available to be shown to other people.

There are no innocent bystanders. Everyone is impacted by bullying. The bystander can be tempted to side with the perpetrator because, perhaps, the perpetrator is in a senior position and therefore has more power.

Perpetrators

It has been suggested that perpetrators bully because of a lack of social competence and a fear of inadequacy, or from motives of jealousy. These three personality traits may be significant, but they are not definitive. Perpetrators are frequently serial bullies. They have got away with it once, so they will do it again. They enjoy the sense of power it gives and the results they achieve. However there will be multiple reasons as to why a perpetrator bullies, never just one reason. In workplaces, including churches, these reasons will almost always include work-related and organisational factors. Where workplaces are going through re-structuring of any sort, bullying is likely to increase because of the fear workers feel about their own employment.

What bullying is not

We all need to be told occasionally when we are not performing as well as we should, or if we have actually done something wrong. This is not bullying; it is the necessary management of individuals. The 'manager' needs to learn how to have these conversations.

Neither does a single aggressive act constitute

bullying. An act of this sort is normally easily recognisable and should always be followed by, at the least, an apology.

Conclusion

Bullying has been shown to be detrimental to the individuals involved, whether targets, bystanders, or perpetrators. It is also detrimental to organisations, in this case the individual church, parish, or parachurch organisation, as well as to the Church as a whole. It damages the Church's mission. If churches – individual congregations as well as whole denominations – are serious about promoting the gospel of Jesus Christ, they must be aware of the damage which is being done by bullying and, in particular, in allowing bullying to continue unchecked.

---

[1] The House of Bishops, *The Mistreatment of Adults by those Authorised by Bishop's License to Leadership Positions in the Church,* (London: Archbishops' Council, 2001).

[2] de Berry, Andrew, MSF Clergy & Church Workers' newsletter, 'Caring for the Carers', 1999.

[3] 'Amicus wins payout for bullied reverend' https://www.tuc.org.uk/research-analysis/reports/amicus-wins-payout-bullied-reverend. 28 July, 2006.

[4] Kennedy, Pauline and Arthur Kennedy, https://www.balmnet.co.uk

[5] Presentation by Canon Bob Baker of Archbishops' Council to St. Albans Diocese on Clergy Terms of Service, 2004.

[6] Rayner, Charlotte, 'From research to implementation: finding leverage for prevention' *International Journal of Manpower, 20,* 1/2, p28, 1990.

[7] Martin, Sheila (2008), Empowering Baptist Ministers who have been bullied in their churches.

3

Trouble at St Chad's

RUTH CARTER

Ruth sets the scene

St Chad's is a church with an eclectic, largely elderly congregation who attend because it is on a bus route and easier to get to than their local parish church. In the late-twentieth century it had a vicar for over 30 years who was very greatly loved. On his retirement the next incumbent stayed for about 10 years, but left following a complete breakdown of pastoral communication and trust. The next incumbent was David, whose wife Ruth had a full-time job. David inherited a number of retired clergy with permission to officiate. One of these, Jason, had assumed most of the responsibility for running the church during the vacancy. Jason and his wife Jean had been part of this congregation for about 5 years. They came from a very different theological position from that of St Chad's. Although Jason told David that he had 'a license to St Chad's', this was not true; he only had general permission to officiate.

Because of their recent history, the congregation was in turmoil. Two weeks before his licensing, a churchwarden visited David and Ruth and told them that Ruth was not welcome in the church because 'Your predecessor was known as "the spy"'. They apparently assumed that Ruth would also function as a 'spy'. It is unfortunate that this did not spur David to turn the appointment down, even at that late stage. At this point, David also discovered that the liturgy in use was one no longer authorised by the Church of England. The bishop quite reasonably asked David to make sure the church used an authorised liturgy within 6 months. Jason started telling members of the congregation that 'David is going to change everything'. This shortly became 'David is continually insulting me'. Within weeks Jason and Jean were also saying 'Ruth doesn't like me', which quickly became 'Ruth hates me' and 'Ruth has long term serious mental health problems' – amongst other things.

Jason had an unusual history. He had never been in charge of a church but had had a variety of other jobs. Jean thought that by marrying Jason she was going to become a vicar's wife. So both Jason and Jean were disappointed people. Jason had helped locally in a variety of parishes, but his relationship with the incumbent invariably turned sour. In one parish, which was a good match theologically, Jason and Jean were asked to leave.

During his first 18 months in post, David became aware of a number of serious problems in the parish including clergy sexual abuse, clergy fraud, and domestic violence. David went to see the bishop and asked him why he had not been told about any of the parish's problems. 'If I had told you, you would not have accepted the job.' Clearly getting a priest in post was more important than having care for one of his clergy couples or giving them any support. When reporting the clergy sexual abuse to the archdeacon, David was told, 'I don't think we need to do anything about this, they are just silly women.' However, David insisted the diocese took the allegations seriously and the clergy person concerned had his permission to officiate removed. After 9 months the bishop wrote to David and said could he give this priest his permission to officiate back and 'put him out of his misery'. No mention was made of giving pastoral care to his victims or of disciplining in any way the priest concerned. David followed all the procedures then in place in the diocese, but had to insist on getting the diocese to follow through.

Ruth's story in her own words

It was difficult going to church that first Sunday, having been told I wasn't welcome. I went in quietly and sat at the back. Nobody spoke to me, though I smiled at everyone I could see. A woman was sitting in the front row who obviously had very severe learning difficulties. She was quite disruptive, constantly turning round and talking to the people behind her. At coffee, after the service, I noticed that people were really nasty to her, saying things like 'you do behave badly in church' and 'your mother didn't bring you up very well'. On week two I went and sat with her and discovered that although she could not read, all she wanted was to be on the right page in the service book. I persuaded her the following week to sit at the back with me. But the constant gossip and undermining, especially of my husband, really got to me. We got to the point that as soon as we got home from church, we had a drink. We quickly realised that we had to stop that. Every time I arrived in church, I could see Jean talking to people and turning round to look at me. After about 10 months David and I thought that the best thing to do would be to ask Jason and Jean what the problem was, why they were saying things about us which were simply not true. We decided to meet at the church – on neutral ground. It was a very, very unpleasant hour. Jason and Jean just shouted at us all the time. Jason accused David of insulting him all the time. When he was asked to give instances, the only thing he could come up with was that in his first month in the parish, David had only asked him to preach once, at evensong, 'when everyone knows the morning service is the main one'. Jean shouted at me 'everybody hates you' – amongst other things. We then discovered that the following day, Jason and Jean had gone to a churchwarden and told them that we had shouted at them for an hour. Neither David nor I had raised our voices at all. Actually I think we were stunned into silence. Now I know that we should never have met with them on our own. It got worse and worse. David met with all the retired clergy in the parish once every fortnight to learn from them and to arrange who would be taking services and preaching. Jason had told David that he was licensed to the parish, so he went to PCC meetings where he constantly criticised David and contradicted him. David spoke to the Bishop's chaplain to ask when Jason's license was due for renewal, to discover Jason was not licensed and never had been. That was the first of many lies which Jason and Jean told us.

This was not a new problem with Jason. He had been asked to leave one church about 15 years earlier, and in every subsequent parish where he helped, there were terrible problems. One incumbent turned to drink (we weren't surprised, we could have done that ourselves). In fact, after about 3 years of hell I was so desperate, I rang the people he had previously 'helped'. I started the conversation saying, 'My name is, my husband is….., I am hoping you might be able to help us with a problem we are having.' Each time the person on the other end of the phone immediately said, 'You are talking about Jason. He is evil.' It was almost uncanny, but I had an identical response from each of them. At least, after those telephone conversations, we felt better. It had happened to other people before us. It wasn't our fault. Ultimately, after another year or so, David had a discussion with the churchwardens, who thought that Jason and his wife were very nice people, and that we were treating them very badly. When asked to give David instances, they couldn't, but said that Jason and Jean had told them various things were happening. David was able to tell them that the incidents they were reporting had never happened. David went to see the archdeacon. He was fairly new, so knew none of Jason's history. However he agreed to invite Jason and my husband to a meeting to try to find out what the problems were. David, on telling me about it later, said that it was the worst hour of his life. Jason just shouted and screamed and hurled abuse at both David and me for a whole hour. Unfortunately the archdeacon did not contact David after this meeting for over a week. It was only a week, but it felt like a month. When he finally wrote to both David and Jason, he said that his advice was that Jason and Jean should leave the church, but he had no power to prevent them becoming members of the congregation.

I can't begin to describe the horrors of the next few weeks. Jason and Jean wrote to all the members of the congregation accusing us of all sorts of things which were completely untrue. Fortunately by this time, the churchwardens had realised things were not as described to them by Jason and Jean and they both supported us publicly. It was announced to the congregation that Jason was leaving the ministry team, though the archdeacon insisted nobody was told that it was on his advice. I think this was wrong. He should have been prepared to stand beside David and explain what he was advising and why. In fact I think it should have been the archdeacon who made that announcement. Two members of the congregation left with Jason and Jean, but everybody else became at least reasonably supportive. And the congregation grew. About 6 months later the archdeacon telephoned David to tell him that Jason had contacted him asking for permission to start a Bible study for the members of

St Chad's congregation. He told David he had no power to stop it, so had given permission. I am really quite angry about that. It was absurd for the archdeacon to tell Jason he could organise a Bible study for people in the congregation he had himself advised Jason to leave.

So it went on, year after weary year. The toll on us as a family was dreadful. At one point I lost my voice for about 6 months, and my husband had a number of health problems. Pastoral support from the diocese to us was totally lacking. Nobody once asked me how I was or what my understanding of the situation was. I was very, very grateful for my job. Nobody asked David how he was or what help he might need. All we had was a great big black hole where support should have been. Total silence. Part of the problem may have been that during this time, all the senior staff in the diocese changed, so nobody had any knowledge of Jason or experience of his previous behaviour. But that is no excuse. The history of a parish is very important. When we finally left the parish, I could not even make myself go inside a church for about two years, nor could I visit the town or our friends there, for many years more than that. I went to a funeral in that church recently, more than 20 years after these events. I could hardly stop shaking. I don't think I will ever recover. It has left me with no trust in church procedures or church people. Fortunately our marriage survived. And our children, having already left home, were okay. But we are both scarred for life. I don't think I will ever trust a bishop or archdeacon again. I could tell you lots more than this, of the awful things that happened, but I think this is the main story.

Names and details in this account have been changed.

4

Hope, Exile and Renewal: A Church of England Curate's Story

JAMES MERTON

'For I know the plans I have for you,' declares the Lord, 'plans to prosper you and not to harm you, plans to give you hope and a future.' (Jeremiah 29:11, NIV)

Hopeful new beginnings

Nothing – not the years of training, the essays, the interviews, or even the confidence and authority the ordaining bishop places in you – truly prepares you for ordination. They call it the ontological shift – a profound change not only in role but in being itself. One moment you are a private Christian, the next you belong to the public. Your faith becomes something expressed in full view – observed, interpreted, sometimes judged.

As I stepped out of the cathedral that afternoon, I felt a clear sense of calling and promise but also vulnerability. Somewhere between awe and apprehension, Jeremiah's promise whispered gentle re-assurance through the noise: *'plans to prosper you and not to harm you, plans to give you hope and a future'*.

I entered my curacy expecting the Church to be a place of holiness, a community of mutuality, a place where the Body of Christ is recognisable in its members. But the Body is both holy and wounded.

After the ordination service, I made my way to my curacy church ready to be welcomed by the congregation in a special service. I arrived excited and nervous in my brand-new clerical shirt and collar. This is it! I was stepping onto the holy ground of living out the ordained life.

Just before the welcome service began, my training incumbent – visibly stressed – strode towards me in the car park and thrust an order of service into my hands saying abruptly 'Read that. It's what we're doing.' I felt affronted, but excused it. Time was short. This was ministry, after all – perhaps just the pace of parish life.

What felt like moments later, I was inside the church for my welcome service, greeted by my new congregation. Midway through the service and without warning, my incumbent announced an 'icebreaker' activity for me – lighthearted in intention, publicly humiliating in effect. I smiled through it, but something in me recoiled. In sacramental theology, outward signs reveal inward realities. This moment, though trivial on the surface, revealed a deeper dissonance.

What followed was a pattern – subtle and overt humour to criticise, to control, to diminish. Sarcasm masked as banter and jokes that cut. At times, others laughed along.

I told myself it was just communication style, that I was being overly sensitive, that this was parish life. But something deeper in me knew this was not right. The holy ground of ordination began to feel like contested territory.

To a place of exile and dislocation

I had expected support, guidance, and encouragement from my incumbent. What I actually experienced felt confusing, corrosive, and quietly soul-wounding.

The move to my curacy parish had been immense – a completely new community, new parish and church, and new home for my family. Everything about our life had shifted and we had invested everything trusting that the curacy would work out well. But there was no safety net or backup plan. The curacy had to succeed.

The dissonance between my outer presentation and my inner reality grew sharper. I could deliver the liturgy, preach with conviction, pray with sincerity – but the still, small voice that once reassured me now wavered in doubt. I began to wonder whether I had mistaken my calling entirely. Was this curacy the wrong fit? Had I misread God's plan? Or worse – had I mistaken my own ambition for divine purpose?

Meanwhile, the dynamic with my training incumbent deteriorated. I became, it seemed, the punchline – the naive curate still learning the ropes, the well-meaning but clueless apprentice. The jokes, the asides, the subtle exclusions – each one chipped away at my confidence. Christian anthropology teaches that every person bears the Imago Dei – the image of God. When someone is belittled, excluded, or controlled, it is not merely a psychological or moral injury; it is a theological one. Harm done to a person is harm done to the image of God within them.

There came a point when the Trojan horse of humour had done its work and I started to retreat.

The energy I once poured into ministry turned inward. Life became about survival, not service. I found myself diminished, slipping off my clerical collar before entering local shops, as though hiding the very identity

I had been ordained to embody. Shame is not a fruit of the Spirit. It is a sign that something in the ecclesial ecosystem has become disordered.

Underneath it all lay a truth few outside the clergy fully understand – the inherent imbalance of power between training incumbent and curate, alongside the fragile vulnerability of the newly ordained. It is fertile ground for power to be abused if unchecked. I do wonder whether the Church fully recognises this dynamic. The system depends on trust, goodwill, and grace. But when that trust fractures, there are few protections. Curates have no employment contract, no real employment rights, no independent grievance process worth the name. They are both student and worker yet belong fully to neither category.

It is a lottery. Some curates flourish under wise and generous mentors. Others, equally called, equally faithful, find themselves diminished, sidelined, or quietly broken. Some simply decide to leave the Church.

A few months into my curacy, the tension between outer composure and inner conflict could no longer hold. I knew something was wrong – not only with what I was experiencing, but with what I was becoming. I was less than I had been called to be.

The diocese, meanwhile, was present but at the same time seemed absent. Yes, there were curate training days and meetings with pastoral 'check ins' but this felt more like performance than places of honesty. The question 'How are you getting on?' routinely asked my curate group by diocesan staff, with what seemed to be polite curiosity, was uniformly answered 'Busy, but good'. No one spoke of problems or personal struggle. There didn't seem to be any issues with our curacies. Ever!

Among curates a year or two ahead of me, there was an unspoken rule: do not cause trouble. If you raise concerns, you become a problem to be managed. And hanging over us all was the quiet but constant threat – that without your incumbent's 'sign-off', your curacy would not conclude and you wouldn't be able to move on. The message was clear: keep your head down and get to the end.

Even though surrounded by parishioners, friends, fellow curates, and diocesan oversight structures, I felt utterly alone.

Eventually, when the internal conflict just became too much, I decided I had to speak up.

I prayed. I took advice. I prepared. My intention in speaking to my training incumbent was not accusation but truth spoken in grace. I told myself that this was not rebellion, but participation in Christ's prophetic ministry. I wanted to be constructive, to own my part, to express concern for our working relationship – not to condemn but to seek understanding. Avoidance was tempting, but my health, calling, and integrity were compromised.

We met in a local cafe. I tried to speak generously. I remember following my notes – careful words about communication and feeling undermined. I admitted my own uncertainty and blind spots. I spoke of wanting to rebuild trust.

She listened in silence, then expressed disappointment and said I was not what she had expected. Very soon afterwards, she ended the curacy.

No mediation. No pastoral conversation. No attempt at reconciliation.

It was a rupture – not only of relationship, but of ecclesiology. The Church proclaims itself a community of forgiveness, dialogue, and mutual discernment. Yet here, the moment I named harm, the relationship was severed. The shock was indescribable. It felt like exile. I had not imagined – not for a second – that the simple act of naming harm could end my curacy overnight.

Looking back, some legal rights would have helped. All curates get is a 'working agreement' – non-binding, largely powerless, often unsigned, and rarely enforced. It is presented as a record of mutual understanding, but it achieves almost nothing. I know curates who never even had one.

The Church would not be compromised by adopting good employment practices: enforceable fair contracts, transparent grievance and tribunal processes, and safeguarding that actually safeguards. The Church should be the safest workplace in the country. Instead, for far too many curates, it is the most precarious.

The only option I had was to make a complaint to the diocese. I still believed that the truth, spoken clearly, would matter. The diocese appointed an external reviewer. The report that followed was polished, pastoral – and, it seemed to me, evasive. On my reading it dissolved responsibility into 'no fault' abstractions: 'communication styles,' 'misunderstandings,' and 'personality differences'. I struggled to see the truth in it.

When I met with the bishop to discuss the future, I was still fragile. She began almost immediately with the question: 'So what have you learned from all of this?' The question carried an implicit theology: that suffering is always formative, that harm is always a lesson, that the wounded must first examine themselves. But Christian tradition distinguishes between redemptive suffering and avoidable harm. Not all suffering sanctifies. Some suffering is simply wrong.

I don't remember what I said in response. Something self-effacing, probably, and not that articulate. The power imbalance in the room was immense. She held my future, my curacy sign-off, and my license in her hands. I was almost completely powerless.

The bishop decided to send me to a new church in a different parish, outside my theological tradition. However the move would split my family. My wife and children had wisely decided to seek sanctuary in a neighbouring church where there were families they already knew. I also knew the vicar. We had met up in the aftermath and shock of my curacy being terminated. He had offered a place of safety and kindness and would be happy for me to join his church to complete my curacy. Out of the wreckage, I glimpsed a path towards renewal.

But the bishop said no.

She insisted I go to her suggested church because it would be 'good for you'. My plea that it would divide the family seemed to be ignored. Recognising my status as effectively powerless, together with the threat of not being signed off, I acquiesced. There were no pastoral considerations, no real consultation, and no sense for me that this was about healing or care.

It turned out not to be good for me at all.

I experienced my new training incumbent as highly controlling. Every movement, every decision, every sermon felt monitored. I learned to stay quiet. Survive the curacy. Get signed off. That phrase – 'get signed off' – became the silent mantra of survival. It became all that mattered.

Even when I had to take time off due to depression brought on by the breakdown of my first curacy, that seemed to be used against me. My new incumbent wanted to extend my curacy because he needed an additional resource for parish work and so he cited a 'gap in my curacy experience and learning'. I fought hard to stop it. My plea to the diocese that the situation was damaging my family again seemed to fall on deaf ears. I distinctly recall a senior diocesan officer saying, 'Extending the curacy is not a punishment, you know', but that's exactly what it was for me. Even the term 'reactive depression' – the phrase used in the report to acknowledge my mental state following the breakdown of my first curacy – seemed to be treated dismissively. 'Oh, that just means a temporary depressive episode', was the passing comment, as though it were no more serious than catching a cold.

The diocesan pastoral structures designed to form and support clergy were now inflicting harm. I had entered ministry to serve the Church and the Church itself was wounding me.

Renewed hope and truth-seeking

And then, quietly and unexpectedly – grace arrived.

An experienced independent person employed by the diocese, tasked with reviewing my curacy file, took the time to read everything properly. She met with me. She listened. She saw what had been happening: the damage, the harm, the institutional indifference. She offered compassion and pastoral concern. She told me she was going to try and help. In her final report to the bishop, she wrote plainly that I had satisfied all the formation criteria and should be signed off.

In Christian angelology, angels are not sentimental figures but messengers – bearers of divine clarity, truth, and protection. They appear when human systems fail, when the vulnerable cry out, and when the truth risks being buried. Her presence felt like a visitation – not supernatural, but sacramental: a human being acting in such alignment with justice and compassion that her work became a sign of God's own advocacy.

It was, at last, a moment of truth. Despite opposition from my second curacy incumbent, the bishop did finally sign me off. I had given her a clear choice though: sign me off or I resign. I am not someone who would normally contemplate issuing ultimatums. It's not me, but by that point I had just had enough. Soon after I left my curacy – battered and bruised, with a deep mistrust of the institution of the Church.

I share my story to raise awareness and in the hope of reform and cultural change.

Bullying happens in the Church and in my experience, it is surprisingly widespread.

But why?

I think there are a few things going on. Firstly, there seems to be a prevailing culture of denial – the unspoken assumption that it couldn't possibly happen here. This is the Holy Church! But the refusal to see what is before our eyes is not holy living – it is avoidance and a failure of ethical and spiritual responsibility.

Power imbalances are also built into Church structures. In Anglican Churches curates depend on incumbents, incumbents on bishops, bishops on archbishops. There seems to be little genuine accountability, and within that hierarchy fear can travel faster than truth. The cost of speaking up can feel too high.

Then there is careerism: the subtle but real competition for recognition, appointments, and promotion. I have seen it first-hand. In a declining institution, where posts are fewer and influence matters more, people can become cautious and self-protective. Reputation management can replace repentance.

The Church of England has also grown accustomed to marking its own homework and resisting external scrutiny. Investigations, reviews, and 'lessons learned' exercises often conclude with no finding of wrongdoing – just 'miscommunication' or 'a clash of personalities'. The result? There is the illusion that institutional harm is minimised. But it is precisely that – an illusion. The damage caused by bullying is profoundly far-reaching, affecting many more people beyond those immediately involved. Ultimately it harms the Church itself.

When I left my second curacy, I told my incumbent that I had a job in chaplaincy. 'Why?' he said. 'Have we put you off parish ministry?' I replied politely that I felt called to chaplaincy work. But I had missed out an uncomfortable truth which was, 'Yes. I have been put off parish work because the institution which should have offered accountability, pastoral support, and truth-seeking has shown me something entirely different.'

The Church cannot keep investigating itself. External oversight is essential – an independent body empowered to review cases, publish findings, and protect those who come forward. In most professions, workers have unions or associations that advocate for fair treatment. The Church could welcome, not fear, similar representation – voices that strengthen rather than undermine the body.

Underlying all the denial, avoidance, and reputation management seems to be fear – fear of exposure, fear of decline, and fear that acknowledging wrongdoing will make people leave. In a Church anxious about its survival, silence can start to feel safer than honesty.

But in our post-truth world, people it seems to me are searching for authenticity – for truth that is lived, not merely spoken. The Church proclaims a crucified God, one who stands with the wounded, not the powerful. Yet too often, the institution aligns itself with self-protection rather than truth.

If the Church is to really tackle its bullying problem, the starting point is basic justice. Curates need more than a non-binding working agreement. They need an employment contract with enforceable legal rights and protections. They also need access to fair, independent resolution processes with legal representation.

Bullying must be named and addressed as misconduct, not hidden behind 'pastoral concerns' or internalised by the newly ordained, too fearful to speak up. And surely it is the case that much could be learned from established and effective anti-bullying practice beyond the Church. In schools and workplaces, listening, recording, and validating experiences are not optional; they are foundational for a healthier culture. Systems of accountability, support, and follow-up are standard. When combined with genuine pastoral care, these practices could transform church culture, making it safe for those most vulnerable and holding those in power to their responsibilities.

God's truth after all is not confined to ecclesial walls. Wisdom belongs to all creation.

We must also examine the theology that shapes our lives and our culture – for when power is confused with authority, or silence with grace, the Gospel itself is at risk of distortion. A Church that fears uncomfortable truth will always end up protecting those with power rather than those who suffer because of it. Too often I have overheard misplaced theological statements around 'service' or 'suffering' or 'formation' which attempt to somehow justify inappropriate and harmful behaviours. I have struggled to see the Gospel in any of it. Sometimes we may need to take a step back and ask ourselves: is love and redemption at the heart of our theology? If not, why not? Power and authority are good and necessary when used, as Christ modelled, in self-emptying service in order for others to flourish.

The Church must learn to listen to the stories it fears – deeply, humbly, and courageously. Prophetic stories of harm and survival are in fact gifts to the Church. They are not complaints to be dismissed, minimised, or managed. As Christ listened to those whom society ignored and marginalised, so the Church must learn to hear those it has wounded.

Those words of Jeremiah 29:11, once a source of unchallenged comfortable reassurance, took on new meaning for me:

'For I know the plans I have for you,' declares the Lord, 'plans to prosper you and not to harm you, plans to give you hope and a future.' (NIV)

They are not words of easy comfort. They were spoken to a people in exile – displaced, disoriented, and holding on to promises that seemed impossible. They are not about guaranteed success but faithful survival. They remind us that even in dislocation, God is writing a hopeful future.

I now understand that my vocation was never only to serve the Church, but to love it enough to speak the truth about it, even when that truth is hard to hear, hard to discern, and hard to voice. But if we can find the moral courage to voice truth or get as close to it as humanly possible, that is where – in my experience – we find the Gospel and the God that transforms.

As you reach the end of this story, pause a moment to listen – not only to what has been said, but to what calls quietly *within you* for a response. Renewal will never be found in silence or avoidance, but in the faithful work of truth-telling and compassionate, grace-filled advocacy. Dietrich Bonhoeffer reminded us that 'not to speak is to speak; not to act is to act'. In that wisdom lies a challenge for every generation, to use our words and our lives in the service of justice and redemption. When truth is spoken in love, when courage and humility meet, the Spirit is given space to reform and renew the Church so that the Gospel can be embodied – transforming not only our lives, but our communities and the world around us.

5

A Question of Trust

JAMES GIBSON

The day that I left the retreat house was heartachingly beautiful. The sea was like a pond, and the warm April sunshine sat in a cloudless sky. However, neither the weather nor the setting reflected the emotional and mental turmoil that I was in.

I had been part of a community for almost 18 months, hoping to live a life of prayer and to support guests at the community's retreat house. The influence and vision of the hermits and desert Christian communities of the third and fourth centuries had been a large part of my spiritual journey for decades.

I was drawn to the retreat house community's spirituality; it purported to be ecumenical and inclusive.

I had previously visited the house frequently, and after a year I felt drawn to the community. I spoke with Robin, one of the wardens, about my sense of calling and they agreed that I should meet with the trustees to discuss it further. It was decided that I could come and live with those involved with the house; my time was to be evenly divided between helping at the retreat house and being a 'prayer presence' who was also available for guests to speak to should they need a listening ear. I was a former psychodynamic counsellor who had also completed the Ignatian Exercises in Daily Life. The Exercises, an intensive process in discernment, involved daily meditation, keeping a daily journal and meeting with my spiritual director every week for a year. I hoped that these skills and experiences would contribute to supporting guests. As a former volunteer and pastoral coordinator at my last church, I also offered to support volunteers, many of them seeking their own spiritual path.

In addition to the wardens, Robin and Chris, who were married, there was a full-time housekeeper called Hilary, a part-time admin worker who also worked in the house, and volunteers. One of the wardens worked full-time in another job so could only commit a limited amount of time. A series of retreats and educational courses were on offer, plus space for those who wanted quiet time alone. We were busy from early March to November.

I arrived in December 2013 when the house was closed to guests, helping me ease in gently. I loved the location of the place and felt deep joy with the wild scenery, the hills and fields, the bird population. I sensed a real connection with God in nature.

It was not until we opened to guests during Lent in 2014 that I began to be concerned about the behaviour of the housekeeper. There were small things, including her being noticeably aggressive towards volunteers and guests. Hilary also claimed that she had not been informed of my role within the community, hence her aggression towards me; I later discovered that she had been told. Being new, I didn't challenge Hilary at first as I was trying to build a relationship with my fellow community members.

Other alarm bells rang when I asked the trustees about safeguarding policies and practices to vet and recruit staff and volunteers. There were none; I was dismayed; this lack of scrutiny applied to everyone involved with the house.

When I asked to be part of the house community, there were no requests for references, nor any criminal records check. No written contracts or job descriptions existed. Safeguarding and HR policies, staff grievance procedures, and disciplinary guidelines were all absent.

I was shocked and offered the trustees ideas for volunteering roles, job descriptions, taking references, and vetting procedures. I raised my concerns directly with Robin and Chris and the chair of the trustees.

Only one trustee acknowledged the need for change and the tightening of procedures; the other trustees, naively or wilfully, did not believe it was necessary.

Some trustees and staff came from an evangelical background and believed that if God was (in their eyes), calling someone to be at the house, then that was all that was needed. I found it disconcerting, given the increasingly bullying behaviour of Hilary and her desire to practise 'deliverance ministry' on anyone who would let her, including guests. She believed the slightest things, such as headaches, were spiritual attacks by Satan and his demons, and that it was her ministry to deliver people from such 'evil influences'.

Experience has shown that retreat centres are often a beacon for people who are vulnerable and lost. Retreatants need nurturing, caring for, and a safe space to explore issues or to be simply left to 'be'.

As a gay man, I was open and honest about my sexuality with the wardens and trustees. Initially I had not told the housekeeper that I was gay; she was not aware of my sexuality. Believing that evil lurked in every corner, Hilary told me openly that she would go into a bedroom previously occupied by people of the same sex and 'cleanse' the room of 'evil-doing and perversion'. It did not occur to Hilary that the occupants might be simply friends or relatives.

Hilary had a strong personality and could walk into a room and change the atmosphere from friendliness to hostility within minutes. She would often pick on trivial things, such as shouting at a guest who had put a mug on the arm of a sofa. She would never admit that she made mistakes and, I found out later, would frequently lie. She certainly exhibited several sociopathic behaviours, and admitted that she never felt empathy.

She would take an instant dislike to someone, often a volunteer, for no reason and bully them. Two guests came to me simultaneously to complain about being threatened and bullied. I told them to speak to one of the wardens, but they felt reticent about doing so as they feared the housekeeper's reaction. I agreed to speak to the warden on their behalf.

When I did this Robin admitted that there had been other complaints over time about the housekeeper. I never found out if Robin did address the issue and I soon discovered that the housekeeper was allowed to do as she saw fit rather than being challenged or reined in. Due to a lack of policies, there was no disciplinary procedure available to address complaints.

There had previously been an incident when I challenged Hilary about her behaviour. I was greeted with floods of tears and extreme hostility. I again spoke to the wardens about this unacceptable behaviour, but they felt that we should sort it out between us without their intervening.

We met and, according to Hilary, she had spoken to Robin and Chris, and was told that it was me who had difficulty fitting in. Several weeks later I challenged the wardens about this, and they were shocked as the housekeeper had blatantly lied. However, they still did not appear to tackle Hilary about her lying.

I discovered that neither the wardens nor the trustees

were able to deal with conflict and would wilfully ignore it. There was a naïve attitude that as we were all Christians, we should live in harmony and 'turn the other cheek', especially within the community. I spoke to the chair of trustees about my growing concerns but like the others, he would not address what was happening.

I would briefly like to explore the bigger picture as I see it. Hilary had a very negative impact on the running of the retreat house; she emotionally damaged guests, volunteers, and staff.

The wardens and trustees seemed to rely on the sense that God was calling an individual to be part of the community. There was no due diligence regarding recruitment procedures, job descriptions, HR issues, and safeguarding policies.

Additionally, if a person of responsibility believed that God was calling someone to join the house community, what were the implications when it was blatantly obvious that said person was causing fear and intimidation? Did that mean that God got it wrong, or would it be possible for the wardens and trustees to admit to themselves that they had got it wrong? Which they certainly did not do. The one trustee who echoed my and others' concerns resigned as they felt it was impossible to persuade their colleagues to deal with the situation.

Contrary to the Articles of Incorporation for the charity, new trustees were invited to join, rather than being elected at an AGM. Trustees' term of office was for three years, unless re-elected for one additional term only, but some would continue long after they should have stepped down.

There was a sense of a collective mindset that resented outside interference. The community had two external 'soul friends', who were engaged to offer practical and spiritual guidance to the community. I had hoped that they would have a more detached view of the situation. However, this married couple were close friends of the wardens and that did not inspire confidence that they would be neutral.

The trustees, wardens, and external soul friends often acknowledged how difficult the housekeeper was to manage, and it was a running joke: 'What has she done now? That's just what she is like.' I had never been in a place where someone was allowed to behave in this way and was not disciplined. She should have been disciplined, supervised closely, or told to leave.

This environment had a direct impact on the wellbeing of some visitors, volunteers, and staff, me included.

In addition, I had to contend with one of the trustees, who was married, telling me how much he was attracted to me and how he often thought of me at night when in bed. I felt extremely uncomfortable, given the power dynamic; he and his wife, also a trustee, were frequent visitors to the retreat house. I often felt cornered and uncomfortable in their presence, yet felt that I had very little say in the matter.

After I left the community in 2015, I felt traumatised by my experience at the retreat house. I had been bullied, yet nobody was listening to my own and others' complaints or was willing to take them seriously. That same year I had to deal with an extremely difficult situation when my mum died of Alzheimer's disease.

Soon after, I began a four-year-long mental health breakdown. I was diagnosed with complex childhood trauma and post-traumatic stress disorder. I had been badly abused by a family member, both physically and mentally.

When in therapy, I learned that I suffered from what is known as 'learned helplessness', a widely recognised psychological theory which addresses the consequences of trauma, including the victim's inability to be assertive and stand up to the perpetrator. It is a way of surviving by metaphorically curling up into a ball to reduce the target area as much as possible when attacked, either physically or emotionally, while being unable to fight back.

I recognised that the situation at the retreat house mirrored my experience of childhood abuse, with my well-being ignored by those who had the power and responsibility to protect me. The trustees, bar one, had refused to acknowledge their responsibilities for the welfare of people involved with the retreat house. It was a collective learned helplessness.

My experiences with the house community left me in a rage with God. I asked how a loving God could allow people, who purported to do things in God's name, to have such a traumatising effect on so many people? I know it is one of the age-old questions of faith, and it severely tested mine.

I stopped praying, did not go to church, and cursed God inside out and upside down. Now that I have regained my relationship with God, I look upon my time over the four years as that of being in a mental, emotional, and spiritual desert. The early desert Christians wrote of being stripped of everything, materially, spiritually, and emotionally, while also wrestling with demons.

An old monk was asked how he dealt with adversity, and he replied, 'I fall down, I stand up and I fall down again, I stand up ...' ... and so on.

Although I would not put myself in the same spiritual league as that of the desert Christians, I now understand that I had endured an experience of 'community' that stripped away my sense of self-worth and awakened flashbacks of childhood trauma. Those I hold responsible for their own cowardice and wilful neglect – the trustees and the wardens – through their inaction damaged not only me, but also many others who sought a place of sanctuary and prayer.

Today I can honestly say that despite my experience of the retreat house, I am standing up again.

Names and details have been changed.

6

Faith, Hope and Disillusionment

EVE FOSTER

Throughout my life as a black lesbian woman, I have had to deal with people's prejudices and bigotry. I have had to face the hurt and pain of exclusion and condemnation a thousand times, as I have searched for those who wish to live the way of peace and love.

I was fostered as a four-year-old and later adopted by a white Christian couple. I was brought up in a predominantly Christian village. No one from the Anglican church there ever made me feel anything other than loved. It was a good life growing up in the church. Even when at twelve years old I made it clear that I was attracted to girls not boys, no one condemned or mocked me. I felt safe.

Today I still live by the same strong moral code that is centred on living with God as my foundation, love as my guide, and kindness in all that I do. It is my constant challenge. My parents taught me the importance of forgiveness, understanding, and love. Do I succeed? No! My actions often fall short. I am a sinner, in thought more than in deed, but a sinner nonetheless. I seek guidance from those who are supposed to know how to help me walk that difficult path without distraction and deviation. I looked to the Church.

Oh, what a terrible idea that was.

The world thirty years ago was a dark place for me. Many held racist and homophobic views and the Church had always been my refuge from hate. For three years I attended the same Anglican church in London. I was an active part of the community, helping with the Brownies and working on the young Christians' team. I made lots of friends, spending time with them outside church.

A gay activist group started holding demonstrations outside churches in the 1980s. They were angry about the Christian anti-gay doctrine. They eventually worked their way round to my church. They say you don't really know people until you go through hard times and challenging situations with them.

Fundamentally, I agreed with the activist group. I knew there was no room for hate in God's house. However, I also had the belief that a place of worship was not a place for demonstrating. I thought about the people in my congregation. They weren't like the anti-gay Christians – after all, they had accepted me.

However, over the following weeks I was to receive a very painful but important lesson. At first members of my congregation started to approach me and question me as to why the demonstrators felt they had the right to disrupt our services and intimidate the arriving parishioners. Some were quite upset and shouted at me. Then they started telling me how outrageous *we* were. I, in complete frustration, went to the minister to appeal for his support. The minister suggested that I might be happier in a different church.

I misunderstood him and I told him that this was my church, I didn't want to leave. I wanted him to talk to the congregation.

He sighed and simply said, 'I feel that this congregation

would be better served if you attended another church. You can leave the church hall keys with me.'

I still can't find the words to express how that made me feel. I was devastated; this was my minister. For three years I had been an active participant in this church. The only time I had asked for anything, I asked for help, assuming the minister would see I had done nothing wrong. I was so shocked. Tears welled up in my eyes and I truly felt my heart break. I felt sick. The only constant in my life was my church family.

I had been raised to know that God loved me without limits and this minister was telling me, 'Not here. God's love is not here for you.' Who on earth gets thrown out of a church? I had sat in the pews alongside thieves, adulterers, liars, and abusers, all God's children, all welcome. But this minister was saying 'not you'. I am a believer, I try to live an honourable life, I help whenever I can. I do not sit on the sidelines, I'm a contributor. I worked hard to assist my church community. So how could this be happening?

I was angry with the group, furious with my church, and positively seething with God.

My biological mother made me and threw me away and it was happening all over again. There was no place in my heart for a God who made me and threw me away. Battered and bruised, I turned away from the Church.

Over the years, as I moved around the country, I would convince myself that it would be different this time. I thought I would find a church that wouldn't judge me. As I continued with my search, I discovered that it took, on average, about six weeks for me to feel the extent of the 'atmosphere'; sometimes from individuals but, more often than not, from groups. It was usually expressed with enforced isolation and exclusion. My address was 'accidentally' missed off the postal list so I missed events and trips. I was even given false information. I was told that a Bible study group was to be held on Tuesday night at 6 p.m. I arrived at an empty building, confused. The group had actually met the previous night, on Monday.

Being on the autism spectrum, I am a plain talker. I find hints and innuendo complicated. Every time these things happened, I genuinely thought they were mistakes. However, I did then notice that no one would sit near me, people would avoid me, make excuses, or depart quickly when I approached to talk to them. I was an extremely sociable person in church. It was my safe space, the place where I could be me. The isolation was unbearable, so again I walked away. Demonising, ostracising, and general bullying are emotional abuses that I do not expect to face at church.

Generally, it would take me two years ranting at God in my bedroom before I would try again. The cycle of faith, hope, and disillusionment continued.

When I arrived in Liverpool, I was still shaking from my last 'Christian encounter'. I had attended a beautiful Unitarian church whose congregation had welcomed me with open arms, but it was not my faith and left me spiritually unfulfilled. I had returned to an Anglican church and, given my history with Anglicans, was feeling like I should seek counselling as I was clearly displaying masochistic tendencies.

Liverpool was my new start. I had a young child. It takes so much energy to raise children. I needed to remain strong and confident. Church was not my first thought. I wasn't strong enough for another round in that ring, my head was still spinning from the last beating.

It was not until my youngest daughter went to nursery that I met a woman who would become the catalyst for my return to church. As our children became firm friends, so did we. When my friend's child was diagnosed with autism it became clear that she would need to go to a caring senior school. When we researched schools for our children, the local all-girls church school was the best and safest option for a mainstream senior school for her child. My three school-aged children were following each other through a different senior school. Although we would both have categorised ourselves as Christians, neither of us was attending a church at that time. My friend asked me to go with her to a church she had attended in the past. My experience in this church was to be my undoing. I would say that I was generally welcomed by the congregation, with a few negative vibes from a small group. But at this church I faced something that I had not faced before. The moment he set eyes on me the minister placed the sinner's noose around my neck and proceeded to spiritually strangle me. Oh, this was new, something I had never faced in a church. As the shepherd leads his flock, the minister leads his parishioners. The minister had identified a black sheep in his flock and he was determined to make sure it got lost.

He was overtly unfriendly. He avoided even the basic greetings and farewells, making sure I felt unwelcome. He was an older traditional man who believed very much in working closely with his flock. He was a leader, and he was fairly good at it. Those who did not follow made excuses for him but did not dare challenge his lead. They knew what he was doing was aimed at me and they knew that it was wrong. Many of them said so, but that is as far as it went. They tried to reassure me: 'Oh, don't worry about him, Eve.' 'Ignore him, he doesn't mean you.' My favourite being: 'He will be retiring soon.'

Although I appreciated their efforts, the minister continued to take every opportunity to undermine, criticise, and condemn. Directly to my face and from the pulpit, he continued to preach about the sin of homosexuality. The minister would wave his arms around, emphasising his points and looking directly at me. Going to church reminded me of being back at school, taking a deep breath before walking in, and taking the continuous beatings, both emotional and physical. Bullies are the same the whole world over, they berate you and encourage others to do the same. They put you down, making you feel less than a person.

I had been taught that the Christian way to behave was never to walk past a person in need or allow an injustice to happen. But here in this church everyone watched while the minister bullied me relentlessly. The congregation witnessed it and did nothing, thereby legitimising his behaviour and leaving me feeling betrayed, alone, and resentful.

I offer no excuse for my reactionary behaviour. I slipped back in time to the school playground and came out fighting. Not with fists but with words. I made a point of engaging the minister in conversation in open church, where it was harder for him to ignore me. I would make good suggestions in meetings, knowing full well he would struggle to find a way to object but would do so anyway. Over time I recognised how uncomfortable I made him feel. My spiteful, angry soul decided it was time for payback. I turned up to everything, every single event, no matter whether it interested me or not. I made sure he felt my presence. A smiling assassin, I became someone I didn't recognise. The promise of his retirement soon was not enough to curb my behaviour. I was going to church but I was further away from God than I had ever been. I was going to church to spite the minister. I was not very proud of myself.

I walked away from that church after attending for seven years. Going to church had again led me away from love. The way I felt about myself and who I had become,

I was sure this was to be my last church. I cannot tell you the relief I felt when I made the decision not to go back. It was like a weight had been lifted and I could start being me again.

Church is supposed to be where we are closest to God, with the other members, no one individual more important than anyone else. We are ALL God's children. Well, heterosexuals are all God's children – the rest of us can go to hell.

Names and details have been changed

7

Bullied into Silence

ANNE SAMUELS

In October 2016 I made the momentous decision to report to the Catholic Church the abuse by a priest which I had suffered over 30 years earlier. I came forward as a committed Catholic, involved in my parish and Head of R.E. in a large Catholic secondary school. I had no idea that 5 years later I would be left feeling totally betrayed by the Church I belonged to, and bullied out by the very institution I thought would care about me.

At the age of 15 my life changed forever. A charismatic priest in his late thirties began to work his way into my circle of friends, teenagers meeting as a music group in our local parish. Several of us were in awe of him. He seemed to be such a spiritual and caring leader and all of us were keen to spend time with him. Little did we realise the motivation behind his friendliness.

I began to get to know him through going to confession. Many years later I would look back and see that this was the beginning of a deliberate grooming process. Invitations to the Priory for meals where I was given alcohol; lifts home late at night; invitations to go swimming; all meant spending more and more time with him. I felt special that I was being included in his life. What I didn't realise was that my life was being stolen. In the swimming pool he used the opportunity to begin to sexually abuse me. He never spoke about what was happening and I knew I was not supposed to talk about it. He had already groomed my family and friends and the abuse couldn't be spoken of. With the skill typical of those who groom children, he gradually progressed the nature of the abuse and by the time I was 18 I was well and truly under his control. It seemed impossible to assert myself or extricate myself from the situation. When I went to university I asked him to leave me alone, but he offered to help my parents by taking me to university at the beginning of terms and collecting me at end. Once I was back in my hometown and teaching, I wrote to him and asked him to stay away. He came to my flat and raped me. The light went out in me. He had completely stolen my sense of personhood and it would take many years of psychotherapy to regain any sense of autonomy.

As a consequence of the abuse, my relationship with the Catholic Church was a complicated one. There was a constant anger bubbling under the surface but at the same time my personal faith and professional life kept me in the Church. My abuse had been the actions of one man, and for some time I was able to separate that from my involvement in my local parish and my work in Catholic education. It was only many years later, after the death of my mother in 2015, that I reported the historical abuse to the Church. I discovered that the Church as an institution was also an abuser and a bully. It was then I had to question my belonging to it.

When my mother died I found it hard to cope with my grief. The outpouring of emotion connected to my relationship with her led me back to those years as a teenager when I had not been able to confide in her. Flashbacks of the abuse and my abuser began to disturb me after many years of coping relatively well. I realised that to have some real sense of peace and healing I needed to report to the Church what had happened to me all those years ago. I was also driven by the fact that my abuser was still in ministry as a parish priest.

And so began the nightmare of re-abuse and re-traumatisation. I approached the Church hoping for healing and closure: I was met with suspicion and disdain. I believed that I belonged to the Church, but was treated as an outsider. The Church, which claimed to live by gospel values, had no room for those who came looking for compassion and support. Instead of reaching out, it closed ranks and used its lawyers and insurers to intimidate me and block me at every step of the journey upon which I was embarking.

When I asked to meet with the safeguarding personnel dealing with my case, I was met with obstacle after obstacle. There was little evidence of care for a survivor; instead, bullying tactics were used against me. Conditions were put on any proposed meeting. I would have to agree to a representative of the priest's religious order being present. When I suggested this was a step too far for me in terms of coping, I was told they were acting on legal advice. Further concerns were met with an email from the Episcopal Vicar for safeguarding asking me to put my complaints in writing. I asked to discuss my concerns with the Episcopal Vicar rather than make a formal complaint; he refused my request. He never spoke to me on the phone or met with me, but when I later made a subject access request I discovered that he had referred to me as manipulative and someone not to engage with 'if you want to get rid of her'. I also discovered that in emails among safeguarding staff I was being described as 'manipulative' and 'needy'; they should 'keep playing the good practice card with' me to control my behaviour.

This was the picture of me which continued to be painted by the diocese. It highlighted the victim blaming culture in the Church: victims and survivors are seen as nuisances and a threat to the Church's reputation and assets. The Church is prepared to use its power to bully us and silence our voices. In my dealings with the diocese there were many times when they tried to control the narrative of what was happening to me. I had given, in good faith, a detailed statement of the abuse I had suffered over many years. This was to be used as an integral part of a risk assessment to be carried out on the abuser by a forensic psychologist. The Church had happily taken all that information from me and yet, without a battle, I would never have known what the outcome of the risk assessment was. This was a real low point in my dealings with them. How could they take so much from me and give nothing in return? The power dynamics put me once more in the position of the abused. The refusal to share information with me was always backed up by the argument that they had taken legal advice. It was only due to the intervention of the forensic psychologist, who challenged the diocese and the religious order to show an ounce of Christian compassion, that eventually I was given some verbal feedback on the risk assessment. It was the psychologist who told me that my abuser admitted everything I had written in my statement: otherwise I would not know to this day that my abuser had admitted his crimes.

In a state of bewilderment and disbelief as to how I was being treated by Church safeguarding personnel, I decided to write directly to the Cardinal Archbishop, believing that I would be met with a pastoral and compassionate response. I was to be proved wrong in this also. The Archbishop was not interested in meeting me or in listening to me. He was quite willing to be a bystander in the nightmare that I was now living. I was later to discover that he had emailed his private office to confirm that he was not going to engage with me. His private secretary suggested that I go back to the Catholic Safeguarding Advisory Service to resolve my issues. But I had already met with them and they had told me that they had no jurisdiction over individual dioceses. I was being sent from pillar to post. It was not until a journalist for one of the national Sunday papers published an article about my case and the unwillingness of the Cardinal Archbishop to meet me, that he eventually agreed to do so.

When I came forward in 2016 to report my historical abuse to the Church, I thought I was engaging with an organisation characterised by a demonstration of gospel values. I was hoping for healing and for justice. Instead there began a journey into the dark side of the Catholic Church of which the majority of its members are totally unaware. It reminded me of the experience of the journalists in the famous film *Spotlight* who uncovered the abuse scandal in Boston. Sadly, it is a story common to most survivors. The reliance on lawyers to shape the Church's response to victims and survivors seems to be its default position – even when there has been no legal claim initiated against the Church.

We have heard many times from bishops and cardinals asking forgiveness, and giving their pledges that things will improve in the future. This was how the Church acted in the past, they say – but the reality is that the Church is acting this way now, in the twenty-first century. For the Catholic Church in England and Wales there are agreed protocols for dioceses and religious orders responding to claims of child sexual abuse. The document, issued by the Catholic Safeguarding Standards Agency in July 2021,[1] clearly states the role and power of the insurers:

- pastoral, spiritual, or other support for a victim or survivor making a claim should only be facilitated after consultation with insurers;

- acknowledgements and apologies are to be considered only after having consulted insurers;
- insurers shall have absolute conduct and control of all proceedings;
- dioceses and religious orders are not to take any steps without specific instructions in writing from the insurers, and are not to give any information about or assistance with a claim to any person claiming against them.

There has to be a point at which the pastoral response supersedes the insurers' response. Bishops and cardinals are asking victims and survivors to come forward, but there should be a health warning about what this will involve.

The Diocese told me on numerous occasions that they had to take legal advice and were in conversation with the head of the Catholic Insurance Service. This company in the UK is a service owned by the Conference of Bishops in England and Wales and of Scotland. It acts as an intermediary for the Church with insurers and also offers legal advice. It was the legal advice coming from the Catholic Insurance Service, owned by the Conference of Bishops, that was driving the direction of decisions in my case. There were no pastoral or Christian responses and, at this stage, I had not begun any litigation against the Church. I simply wanted to be listened to.

I am in contact with survivors now whose lives are on the edge because they cannot get from the Church the pastoral response that they deserve. People in safeguarding positions seem powerless to decide to do the right thing. Until that is known and brought out into the light of day; until the laity understand that the money they put into the collection is funding the Church's use of lawyers and insurers in this way, there is little hope of any cultural change. The Church desperately needs leadership that is prepared to put its head above the parapet, stand up to the bullies, and answer the question, 'What would Jesus do?'

I wrote to the Cardinal Archbishop in the summer of 2021 when more untruths written in emails about me had come to light, and his lawyers were saying that I had no right to speak about it. I asked him, 'What would Jesus do?' His response was, 'The safeguarding office and the chief operating officer are the people dealing with your case.' Despairing of those at the top ever taking responsibility, I decided to play them at their own game. I took legal action against the diocese for the way in which their response to me had re-traumatised and re-abused me. The diocese settled my claim out of court in October 2021.

Bishops, cardinals, the Pope, can make as many statements as they like about how the Church is changing. But until they take responsibility for decisions about how they are going to respond to victims and survivors, and they are no longer willing to leave those decisions to insurers and lawyers, there will be no change and victims and survivors will have to continue to battle against being bullied into silence.

'Anne Samuels' is not the author's real name. She was witness A711 at the Independent Inquiry into Child Sexual Abuse. Details of her story have been changed.

---

[1] This document has since been removed from the Catholic Safeguarding Standards Agency website. It is not known whether the policy is still being implemented.

8

'My Life Will Never Be the Same': The Psychodynamics of Workplace Bullying and the Inner World of the Bully

FIONA GARDNER

In January 2010 the *Church Times* published a number of disturbing letters on bullying as endemic in the church. One correspondent, name and address supplied but not published, included the following in their letter:

> 'It is quite ridiculous for some of our bishops to state that bullying does not occur in the Church of England ... I was put through nine months of sheer terror, which resulted in my trying to take my life on two occasions ... My life will never be the same. I still open mail with terror, and cannot attend diocesan occasions through fear.'[1]

Other correspondents cited the difficulties and repercussions of whistle-blowing, lack of legal or pastoral support, the damage done to faith in God and the Church, the protection of the bully by the structures of the Church, and problems linked to losing accommodation as well as the job.

Twelve years later Paul Skirrow, a priest in retirement, suggested that despite Church of England policies and training programmes to deal with bullying it has become embedded as part of the very structure, systems, and culture of the Church, and in the normal practice of management. So much so that:

> ... it is difficult to pinpoint and identify a practice which is diffuse and permeates a whole system, and it is the nature of such a system that it is far from easy or safe for an individual to make a stand when isolated.[2]

Paul Skirrow used as his definition of bullying: the abuse and mistreatment of someone vulnerable by someone stronger, more powerful. He saw the very structure of the Church as characterised by institutionalised bullying.

This chapter examines the psychodynamics of bullying from a triadic perspective involving the inner worlds of both bully and the person being bullied, and also the organisational culture of the Church of England. To illustrate, an example of bullying between a training incumbent and her curate is used:

> *Clare is a long-standing vicar in a small town and Sarah was placed there as curate. Both women are middle-aged with Clare a few years older. Sarah had previously worked as a social worker, and her apparently easy ability to relate to the parishioners complemented Clare's more intellectual and detached personality – Clare is also a perfectionist. Initially there was a good relationship between them, but*

gradually tensions and difficulties emerged. These were exacerbated by Clare's irritation about how after the main Sunday service Sarah, positioned in the porch, would build up a queue of people wanting to talk with her, while Clare was left outside briefly shaking hands and complaining of the cold. Clare's growing resentment at feeling that the parishioners liked Sarah more than her, led to her increasing pressure on, and criticism of Sarah. This began with extra demands and quibbles about what Sarah had or hadn't done, escalating to direct criticism of her abilities to fulfil her curacy. Sarah, outwardly confident but inwardly full of self-doubt, felt inhibited in relating to parishioners, and increasingly anxious to placate Clare. Eventually the pressure contributed to several serious mistakes culminating in Sarah taking prolonged sick leave.

The inner world of the person who is bullying

It is clearly helpful to take a broad range of potential causes of bullying into account, which may lie within the organisation, the perpetrator (the bully), the social psychology of the work group, and also the victim. Studies on the personality of the person who bullies have identified what has been described as the dark triad of adult bully syndrome: narcissism, entitlement, and callousness. These traits become exemplified through controlling and manipulative behaviours designed to inflict psychological angst or even physical harm on others in the workplace. The typical bully is not psychologically well adjusted, often has problems in his/her home life, cannot handle emotions, and has little empathy for others. These aspects sit uneasily within the Christian context where the shadow or negative is often denied and positive traits exaggerated. How and why such characteristics develop deserves a deeper understanding, and this can be examined in looking more deeply at Clare's inner world.

What is clear in the example of Clare's bullying behaviour is that she felt threatened by Sarah and her self-esteem was wounded by Sarah's apparent popularity: so much so that Clare began to use all possible means to defend her position; suggesting that her self-esteem was vulnerable, and her ability to self-reflect lacking. Clare later admitted that she had felt envy, implying that Clare – despite her intellectual capabilities and apparent detachment – felt less worthy and less deserving than Sarah. Why would this be? Clare grew up with two younger siblings: a brother whom she was able to exert her will over and control, and a younger sister – a child much favoured by the parents. Clare as she grew up struggled to gain her parents' interest and approval, eventually being seen as the 'clever' one, whereas her younger sister was recognised as prettier and more likeable and even-tempered. The powerful dynamics of sibling rivalry were evoked every Sunday by the scene in the church porch. Clare believed that she deserved better, but her sense of self-worth was heavily dependent on external validation. Her favourable view of herself was contradicted by what she saw as her unpopularity over Sarah's popularity, despite all the work she had put into the parish over many years. This threatened sense of self – her wounded narcissism and her sense of entitlement – led to aggression and callousness in her actions towards Sarah. Her perfectionism, a quality developed in childhood from trying to gain parental love, became tyrannical and uncontrollable and was projected onto Sarah whom she criticised over the slightest mistake.

For some time, Clare could not reflect on what had happened, and repeatedly claimed that she was not aware of the consequences of her behaviour and how badly Sarah had been affected. Initially defensive, she saw it as a reasonable reaction to what had felt a tense situation, in part explained by her own responses to increasingly weighty responsibility for the parish fuelled by diocesan initiatives. Clare's wider responsibilities are discussed in the next section.

The organisational culture

The concepts of power and control are essential to understanding workplace bullying where, as with Clare and Sarah in the positions of training incumbent and curate, there is an obvious imbalance of power associated with control over Sarah's future career in the church. The actions and reactions to an abuse of power then need to be understood within the immediate context in which they take place. In such a situation it is often difficult for the curate to speak out, and defend herself against the injustice of the training incumbent's actions.

The parish church is also part of the wider organisational culture of the institutional Church and this too, in this example, played a part in engendering the bullying. Ironically, although Clare would not have called it bullying, she too felt under immense pressure. With a dwindling, rather older congregation she was being encouraged to raise attendance and develop initiatives that could draw in a new demographic: young families and youth. Previous attempts had not resulted in much, and Clare felt responsible and inadequate compared to fellow clergy running apparently bigger, more successful churches who she felt criticised her. She had hoped a curate might help with this and bring in new families, and felt irrational frustration at Sarah's over-involvement with the very elderly.

Interesting research shows that even if perpetrators have some common personality characteristics making them prone to bullying, they will not exhibit such behaviour unless they are in an organisational culture that rewards, or at least is permissive of, such behaviours. Some organisations not only create the conditions that enable bullying, but also encourage it. The institutional Church is founded on hierarchical structures and systems of dependency based on power and control.[3] From this perspective, the psychodynamics between victim and bully are played out within a larger frame where self-awareness, self-agency, and reflectiveness become impaired by the force of the authoritarian structure. Whilst the Church does not consciously encourage or condone bullying it has, as Paul Skirrow notes, developed ever more encroaching management practices designed to manipulate a weakened clergy in order to force them to do what the hierarchy wants, through the structures the hierarchy controls. This is the practice of the powerful dominating weaker and more vulnerable people. The hierarchy are engaged in bullying even without their activity being identified as such by them or others. This was the culture that Sarah entered for her curacy.

The inner world of the person who is being bullied

Reflecting on the personality of the person who has been bullied is not about 'blaming the victim' nor about explaining the behaviour of the bully, but it may be relevant in explaining perceptions of and reactions to workplace bullying. It has been found that those bullied in the workplace often have a general tendency to avoid conflict together with a lack of conflict management skills: in other words they have little confidence in handling what is happening. Other studies suggest those who are bullied tend to be conscientious, taking everything very seriously, and often have a negative attitude to humour – especially at work. They may have unrealistic beliefs about the work, believing it will be the ideal position, and so there is difficulty in adjusting not only to the imperfections of the situation, but also to their own part in it. These personal characteristics are not a general explanation of bullying, nor do they undermine and change the responsibility of managers and employers in the prevention and management of bullying in the Church as workplace.

Sarah felt dependent on Clare's goodwill and was very keen to make a success of her curacy. Feeling called to her new vocation she felt confident in the skills she could bring from her work as a social worker with the elderly, but less confident in involvement in new initiatives for young families. It felt familiar to listen to the older members of the congregation and so she rather took refuge in this aspect of the work – not realising Clare's growing fury. When she did realise, her natural response was to placate and become very compliant, wanting to be a loving Christian. She anxiously tried even harder – thus unfortunately repeating her relationship with her own critical mother. Given her mixed feelings this inevitably led to mistakes being made, so increasing the criticism from Clare – a familiar cycle from Sarah's past. It wasn't until she became so nervous that she had to take sick leave, that she allowed herself to recognise the months of bullying behaviour.

The power imbalance contributed to infantilising Sarah, who then felt unable to defend herself or to escape. She was left upset, threatened, humiliated, and vulnerable, and experiencing anxiety, depression, and, confusion about her vocation.

Concluding thoughts

The very structure of the Church is recognised as creating the social architecture for workplace bullying: explicitly through condoning power and control in its hierarchical structures; and implicitly through its culture of dependency. In that sense the institutional Church both provides a blueprint (despite initiatives against bullying), and becomes complicit in what is termed 'bystanding'. This is where the bystander is defined as an active and involved participant in the social architecture of bullying rather than a passive witness.

In the Church, bullying can be redefined as a triadic (bully-victim-bystander) rather than dyadic (bully-victim) perspective. In the Church, bullying is not merely about separate, isolated instances involving the personality of the bully and the relationship between the bully and the bullied, but rather as a dysfunctional solution or even an adaptation which keeps a larger and more meaningful problem unseen: a problem in the heart of the authority structure of the system.

---

[1] https://www.churchtimes.co.uk/articles/2010/15-january/comment/letters-to-the-editor/there-are-clear-instances-of-bullying-in-the-church-of-england-say-victims

[2] Skirrow, Paul, 'Bullying in the Church of England – Personal or Institutional?', In *Surviving Church* http://survivingchurch.org/2022/03/ 18 March 2022.

[3] Gardner, Fiona, *Sex, Power, Control: Responding to Abuse in the Institutional Church* (Cambridge: Lutterworth Press, 2021).

9

The Traumatic Impact of Bullying

RHONA KNIGHT

Overview

This chapter explores how bullying in church contexts can traumatise individuals, communities, and congregations, and how poor and inadequate institutional church responses can compound traumatic experience, increasing the likelihood of Post-Traumatic Stress Responses.

Traumatic experience is a deeply disturbing event or series of events that overwhelms an individual's or congregation's ability to cope. Post-Traumatic Stress Disorder (PTSD) is a medical diagnosis describing specific, ongoing symptoms and impacts of the traumatic incident(s). While few go on to experience PTSD, a significant number experience symptoms which, while not meeting the diagnosis threshold for PTSD, are common and clinically significant. The terminology and definition of this sub-threshold PTSD are still emergent. I will call these Post-Traumatic Stress Responses (PTSR).

Bullying behaviours here will be limited to those identified in Einarsen et al's Negative Acts Questionnaire. To protect anonymity, composite examples will be used to illustrate bullying behaviours. The term 'target' will be used to describe the person being bullied. Mobbing describes bullying by a group.

What do we know?

Bullying in children can result in traumatic experience for the person being bullied and long-term adverse effects in the perpetrators of bullying and in those who were bystanders.[1] The last four decades have seen increasing acknowledgment of, and research into, the traumatic impact of bullying, mobbing, and victimisation in work settings. Aristidou et al demonstrated greater severity of trauma symptoms in those who: are bullied more; also witness bullying; perceive reporting the bullying to be unimportant; have considered resigning their post. They concluded, 'both victims and witnesses of workplace bullying/mobbing need to be assessed by mental health professionals for PTSD ... symptoms in order to have access to effective treatment'.[2]

Leymann and Gustafsson evidenced severe PTSD in people experiencing workplace mobbing. A meta-analysis (Nielsen et al) identified that while bullying is a prevalent traumatic stressor in workplaces, there is not yet enough evidence to *causally* link bullying with PTSD. Spence, Laschinger and Nosko found not only that workplace bullying appeared to be linked to PTSD, but that psychological capital (hope, optimism, efficacy, and resiliency) has only a limited effect in mitigating the adverse responses. In experienced nurses, only efficacy was found to moderate the bullying/PTSD relationship. While studies to test the causal link between workplace bullying and PTSD are sadly lacking, the evidence does seem to indicate a correlation between the two.

Trauma is held in the body

The part of the nervous system that is continually keeping us alive is the autonomic nervous system. It is made up of two parts that 'dance' together, each part responding in different ways to the demands of daily life. The 'parasympathetic' dance partner is generally more active but is suppressed in times of acute or longer-term stress. The 'sympathetic' dance partner is generally less active but becomes more active if there is a stress to deal with. If there is a sudden shock the increased activity of the sympathetic dance partner results in increased heart and breathing rates, tense muscles, and butterflies in the stomach. Trauma sets our autonomic nervous system into chaos. In times of significant threat, bodies can move into flight, fight, flop, or freeze response modes, depending which dance partner is triggered to be most active at the time. Trauma also impacts on the brain, such that memories are not processed properly, perceptions of risk are altered, and particular experiences can trigger post-traumatic responses. Someone who has been traumatised by church-related bullying is at risk of PTSR. Triggers might include seeing someone in a dog collar, a piece of church liturgy, or even smelling incense. The nervous system slips into chaos again, as the person's body responds as if they were once again in that place of trauma.

Trauma can also be experienced by congregations and communities. The Tragedy and Congregations[3] project has gathered together resources and research on communal experiences of trauma, including a model of the normal journey through communal trauma. Heroic, disillusionment, rebuilding, and restoration phases culminate in a wise-living phase that equates to the post-traumatic growth phase of individual trauma. Take, for example, the new church leader who has a bullying manner and demonstrates bullying behaviours. The impact of these behaviours will be on individuals, but also will have a ripple effect on the wider church community. In his exploration of the theological and ethical issues of bullying, Andrew Goddard notes how the character of a leader shapes the wider culture and ethos of an organisation, with the 'damaging effects not just on those directly subjected to the bullying but much more widely, including giving licence to others to bully'.

Bullying and trauma triggers

Traumatic experience is made more likely where people are exhausted. It can result from a one-off significant bullying event, such as being attacked in the church by an angry or unwell parishioner; having a ministerial license revoked with no reason or justification; being shouted at aggressively by a church warden in a PCC meeting; or a physically intimidating sexual advance from a bishop.

It can also come as a result of longer-term, more subtle behaviours. Less obvious, ongoing bullying behaviours can erode and corrode until eventually a small one-off incident becomes the last straw. Serene Jones notes that while this low-grade behaviour pattern 'never reaches the explosive level of violence we associate with traumatic harm, its corrosive effects are more likely to go unnoticed – and uninterrupted – for years'. Such bullying behaviours might include rumours being spread by members of the church about a church leader; unchecked cyber-bullying through emails and online platforms like Facebook and X; a training minister micromanaging the work of the youth pastor; gaslighting. Gaslighting is a subtle form of manipulative bullying which can result in the person questioning what has happened and their understanding of it.

Bullying as abuse

To enable a framing of abuse, including bullying and mobbing, I have developed a six-category approach which I term the Abuse Categorisation Tool (ACT),[4] in which we ask six questions:

1. Who is being abused?
2. Who is perpetrating the abuse?

3. What is the context of the abuse?
4. What method is being used to abuse?
5. What is the impact of the abuse?
6. What factors are enabling the abuse?

Consider Eli's story of traumatic abuse:

Eli comes from a UK multi-ethnic background and is a curate in a city church. Following a happy and successful senior management role before training for ordained ministry, she settled well into curacy, but has noticed recently that her training incumbent has decreased the number of services she is leading or preaching in and has not included her in relevant emails and meetings. She also feels that she is being undermined and placed in difficult positions by her training incumbent. In one of the recent school Christmas services, he asked her to lead prayers at short notice and then made a public derogatory comment about her. One of the parishioners mentioned to Eli that her training incumbent has told him that Eli is difficult to work with. Having been a confident person, Eli is now finding herself feeling fearful and ashamed, wondering how much more she can take and is considering whether she should really be in ordained ministry. She is even finding prayer difficult. She is sleeping badly and feels anxious most of the time. A friend has commented that Eli is becoming more isolated. Eli has spoken to the rural dean, who has indicated she would be wiser getting on with it all and not complaining.

Using ACT, we would see that:

1. Eli is the target of the abuse.
2. Her training incumbent is perpetrating the abuse.
3. The context of the abuse is curacy.
4. The method of abuse is bullying behaviours:

Information is being withheld that is affecting her performance

Her opinions are being ignored

She is repeatedly being given tasks with unreasonable deadlines

She is being humiliated in connection with her work

She is being ignored and excluded

Rumours and gossip are being spread about her

She is receiving signals that she should leave her job

5. The impact of the abuse is:

Physical – she is not sleeping and has lost weight

Emotional – she is feeling anxious most of the time

Spiritual – she feels ashamed, finds it difficult to pray, and is questioning her call

Social – she is becoming more isolated

6. Factors enabling the abuse include:

Poor training incumbent selection, training, and quality assurance

Lack of clear diocesan pathways and processes

Passive bystanders, in the parish and the diocese

Two months later, Eli is leading evening prayer. At the end of the service the training incumbent tells Eli off in front of everyone for not using the right readings from the lectionary. Eli leaves the church and arrives home two hours later, unsure how she has got there. The impact of this final act has tipped Eli into a dissociative traumatic response.

The outcome of Eli's story – Version 1

Eli is signed off sick. She sees a trauma therapist. She meets with the new archdeacon twice and is listened to fully. The archdeacon seeks advice and uses a clear bullying policy from another diocese. The allegations are fully and appropriately investigated. The bullying claims are substantiated. Interventions are put in place to: support Eli through her curacy in a different parish; to support the congregation who were adversely impacted by Eli's sudden departure from the parish; to support the training incumbent, who had also been badly impacted by all that had happened. Eli completes a course of trauma therapy and commences a team vicar post in the same diocese. She decides to do a master's degree in conflict resolution and mediation, building on the work she did in that area prior to training for ordination. She hopes this will benefit the wider church and bring further meaning to her trauma.

The outcome of Eli's story – Version 2

Eli is signed off sick. She sees a trauma therapist. She briefly meets with the archdeacon and endeavours to explain what has happened. The diocese does not have or access an effective bullying policy. The archdeacon takes the situation to the bishop's staff committee and it is quickly decided that there is a personality clash. Eli is an 'assertive' woman and it is quite understandable why the training incumbent, who is 'a good egg', behaved as he did. No investigation is done; the congregation and incumbent receive no help. Eli completes her curacy in a different parish where a number of church members are known to disagree strongly with the ordination of women. At the end of her curacy, she is told in writing that her interpersonal skills need more work and that there is no role for her in the diocese after her curacy. Eli begins to experience significant PTSR requiring longer term therapy. Being geographically tied by caring responsibilities, she leaves ordained ministry. The training incumbent's next curate also complains of bullying …

Conclusion

For the traumatic impact of bullying to be minimised we need church organisations that have and model open, transparent, clear, accountable, just, and effective processes to address issues of power misuse and bullying.

The concerns of those who perceive themselves to be targets must be taken seriously, investigated, and addressed, ensuring investigators are free from any conflict of interest. *Appropriate* support and mediation must be enabled sooner rather than later. In this way bullying behaviours can be addressed early, decreasing the likelihood of traumatic experience and PTSR.

Malicious accusations of bullying can often be complex and also require clear, effective processes, to enable them to be identified and dealt with appropriately and in a timely way. The accuser may themselves be demonstrating bullying behaviours, resulting in traumatic experiences for the wrongly accused.

A trauma-informed organisation will realise that, because of the impact of trauma on processing and memory, stories of traumatic experience may well not appear logical or rational. A trauma-informed organisation will also be aware of the ripple effect and the vicarious impact on the wider community.

---

[1] Vanderbilt, D. and Augustyn, M., 'The effects of bullying', Paediatrics and Child Health 20.7 (2010): 315-320. Available at: https://www.sciencedirect.com/science/article/abs/pii/S1751722210000715 (last accessed 23 Oct 2022).

[2] Aristidou, L., et al, 'Association between workplace bullying occurrence and trauma symptoms among healthcare professionals in Cyprus', *Frontiers in Psychology*, 11.575623 (2020): 1-19. Available at: https://www.frontiersin.org/articles/10.3389/fpsyg.2020.575623 (last accessed 23 Oct 2022).

[3] 'Tragedy and Congregations' project. Available at: https://tragedyandcongregations.org.uk (last accessed 23 Oct 2022).

[4] Knight, Rhona, 'Breathe, Eat, Drink: liturgical trauma and the Church of England', presented at The British & Irish Association for Practical Theology (BIAPT) Annual Conference 2022 – Flesh & Blood: Embodiment & Practical Theology.

10

Silencing and Retraumatising

REBECCA PARNABY-ROOKE

'Silence is Golden', as The Tremeloes famously sang. Jazz musician Miles Davis spoke of his craft belonging in the music he did not play; and quotes have been attributed to both Debussy and Mozart speaking of the power of silence in music. The notes you don't play are often as important to a piece as the ones you do.

Think of that moment when a conductor holds the orchestra in position after the final note of a piece. Nobody plays a sound, nobody moves. The music is still being intentionally crafted, as represented by the musicians remaining poised. The art is still in motion. But for that moment, they are allowing the silence to ring out just as powerfully as the notes did moments before. Without that moment, what came before would be diminished.

It is an art, knowing how to craft silence. As music therapists, this forms an essential part of our training. In his excellent blog 'What is Music without Silence',[1] Phil Evans succinctly explains the way we work with silence to support our clients. Specifically he explains. 'Silence in music therapy, as in life, can take on many qualities. It can be oppressive or mutual, uncomfortable or soothing' (Evans, 2013). It is this subversion of silence from the intentional and powerful to the forced and harmful which I seek to explore in this chapter.

Preserving the positive silence

In a music therapy session, if I heard a client play a soft instrument, such as an egg shaker, and responded with a hard strike on a bass drum, it would drown out their contribution, send the message my voice was more important, and discourage them from contributing again. I wouldn't be doing my job. My role within the session is to facilitate the client in communication, musical interaction, and therapeutic development, not to make the musical sounds I like best. So, I may choose to hold my silence and look interested, hold a paused chord to invite more of their sound, or repeat their pattern to show I had heard it. I would acknowledge what they had done musically and give them encouragement to continue sharing what they had to offer.

How often is that the response to a survivor? We hear you, we are interested, please give us more?

Should my response be effective, and the client be in a position where they feel able, we may proceed on a musical journey together, exploring what they have to share. My role now is to facilitate, encourage, and most of all listen. To hold the space for any emotions or challenges we may encounter on the way.

How often is that the experience during a survivor journey? We are here for you; please know you are supported and we will tackle whatever arises together?

Once the moment has run its course, all has been expressed, and we come together in a moment of pause, there will be a silence. An opportune moment. This is the moment in which all that came before can be taken away as constructive, or can be ruined.

How often is it that the meetings had by survivors, which

feel to have been beneficial, are ended with platitudes, broken promises, or inaction?

I treasure that moment of silence, however brief. I invest in that moment of shared understanding, of coming together at the end of an intense journey. For it is always profound when someone chooses to share vulnerability with me. I have a responsibility in that moment to honour their choice, and take it forward with grace and respect. For me, that means recording what has happened in my clinical notes, sharing the event with family or staff teams (should that be appropriate) and ending every session with a 'Thank you' song for the great privilege it has been to be with the client in music.

How often are survivors' experiences respected and centred so? How often are records comprehensively kept, and information appropriately shared in line with GDPR and Caldicott principles? How often are survivors thanked for the great efforts they go to every time they relive their experiences, knowing the cost each time?

What is retraumatising?

The cost of subverting silence is retraumatising survivors. This takes many forms, but first let us be clear with a definition of the term. Retraumatising is defined as 'one's reaction to a traumatic exposure that is colored, intensified, amplified, or shaped by one's reactions and adaptational style to previous traumatic experiences.'[2] Essentially, an event which takes a person back to the state of trauma experienced at a prior time. This is not to be confused with the term 'trigger', which in comparison would be an event which increases a person's emotional response in relation to a state of trauma experienced at a prior time. Put simply, a trigger reminds and therefore evokes. Retraumatising places the person back in the physical, emotional and spiritual state of trauma as a full-bodied response.

It may feel like a bold claim to suggest silence can impact a person to the extent they have a physical response – until we consider the myriad ways silencing can occur, especially in the context of bullying: repeated microaggressions which make a person afraid to speak out, in case their contribution is commented on, ridiculed, or contradicted. Being spoken over or shouted down. Left out of email chains or meetings. Finding out about key issues concerning their work through unofficial channels, removing any opportunity for discussion or feedback – with the refrain, 'Oh, I thought you already knew' echoing though the gossip. As if that would make it okay – the blow had already been delivered and further participation in sharing the news was a mere aftershock.

The earthquake analogy is a good one to use when it comes to trauma and retraumatising. When an earthquake hits you get the initial tremor, registered on the Richter scale and causing various levels of damage. It is a most unsettling thing to feel, an earthquake. During the Market Rasen earthquake in Lincolnshire on 27 February 2008, I was woken from my sleep feeling like I was being thrown around in a snow globe – while still lying on my bed. I have never felt anything like it. But that isn't necessarily the end of it.

Aftershocks can be just as devastating as the original seismic event. Some even register as high on the Richter scale as their original tremor. The aftershocks can keep on coming for days, even years; one series of aftershocks from New Madrid in North America have been active for 145 years – and counting! Not only do they cause damage in their own right, but they destabilise what has been shored up from the previous events. They make already damaged spaces worse. They trigger near collapses to become full destructive events. Just as retraumatising events do for abuse survivors.

Silence, retraumatising and spiritual abuse

Judith Herman describes silent survivors as 'carrying the weight of a burden that does not belong to them'.[3] When the #MeToo movement gained rapid traction on social media in 2017, it was almost as if sexual abuse survivors everywhere were breathing a collective sigh of relief. They could finally lay down the weight of their burdens and relate to people. Use their agency. Share parts of themselves which had never seen the light of day. No longer be silent.

For with silence comes shame.

I cannot talk about this; it must be hidden. I'll be considered dirty, stupid, I brought it on myself.

With silence comes doubt.

Am I a victim, or actually, did I deserve this, were they right, am I wrong, bad, mad? Evil. Sinful.

With silence comes fear.

What if I accidentally talk about anything close to this, and cause trouble. I'd better not talk at all.

With silence comes introversion.

I can't talk about this, so I won't talk about anything. I'm better off on my own.

With silence comes frustration.

Can't people SEE that something is wrong? That I'm hurting? That I'm not ok?

With silence comes anger.

WHY is nobody LISTENING to me? WHY won't someone HELP ME?

When we are forced into positions of silence, all of this confusion, pain and negativity has only one place to go: inwards. We become ashamed of ourselves. Doubtful of our own identity. Fearful of our own judgement. Introvert, unless we use crutches to take us out of our misery for just a short while. Frustrated because we know, deep down, we were made for more than this.

And then comes the anger. Anger because all around us we see the pastors who abused us as children continuing to live out their days free from justice. Anger because we pursue our abusers through the courts, through jury trials where we, as witnesses, are the ones tried and found to be 'not convincing enough' while our rapists walk free. Anger because we lose our health, honour and livelihoods to relentless bullies who use statutes and diktats to trap us in a world of legalism. While we sit, silent, typing messages and deleting them, because 'it won't help our case'.

I often wonder, actually, if it would help our case. If instead of adhering to the social norms of smiling politely and ignoring growing animosity, waiting two months for the next PCC to raise an issue, or subtweeting our grievances without ever making an actual complaint to the person involved, we would actually do better by grappling with the process outlined in Matthew 18:15-17. Speak up, individually, then with trauma-informed, trusted, and suitable supportive peers. Make it commonplace for siblings in Christ to be people who have difficult conversations. Because the harm which comes from fear of speaking up cannot be overemphasised.

In her courageous book *A Spirituality of Survival*,[4] Methodist leader Barbara Glasson talks about the importance of finding a language of inclusion. We can only do that if we make space to listen and truly hear what each person has to say. What one person may see as liberating, another may see as oppressive. We can only begin to understand those dynamics if we name them first, without seeing them as confrontational or personal attacks, just spoken truths from the hearts of beloved siblings in Christ. When we speak into the silence, name our truths, we give each other the power of information. With that, the weight of the burden of silence is lifted.

The shame, pain, and sin is placed back with the one to whom it belongs. Jesus can deal with it there. With us, the process of restoration and reconciliation can begin. Aftershocks can no longer impact the previously damaged infrastructure because instead of being shored up with wood, it is now being rebuilt from the ground up with iron.

We don't know what burdens are carried by those we meet. Some of us may never be able to speak of them. Others may, in time, but not yet. Through my work I have been privileged to enable the breaking of silences which have been held for decades. As people of faith we are called to nurture spaces where all feel able to speak. Where silence is an invitation for glorious sound, not an oppressive, threatening blanket of pressure. Whether through speech, sign, augmentative communication tools, writing, singing, symbols, advocacy, or any other form of expression. We must be open, listening to and caring for what we receive in the space we hold. For what beauty could we be part of if we are?

---

[1]   Evans, P., 'What is Music without Silence.' At https://www.huffingtonpost.co.uk/phil-evans/music-therapy-silence_b_3390764.html Accessed 14th October 2022.

[2]   Danieli, Y., 'Fundamentals of working with (re)traumatized populations' in G. H. Brenner, D. H. Bush, and J. Moses (eds.), *Creating spiritual and psychological resilience: Integrating care in disaster relief work* (pp. 195–210) (Abingdon: Routledge/Taylor & Francis Group, 2010).

[3]   Herman, J. (ed.), *Trauma and Recovery* (New York: Basic Books, 2015), p. 200.

[4]   Glasson, B., *A Spirituality of Survival* (London: Continuum, 2009).

11

Barriers to Addressing Bullying in Congregational Settings

LORRAINE TURNER

No group of people worshipping together would espouse bullying as an acceptable way for Christian people to interact with each other, and yet many different types of bullying occur in churches. This might be between members of a congregation, colleagues in ministry, or between ministers and congregation members. In this chapter, I would like to share my sense of the reasons why this may happen. I will explore ways in which the common human behaviours of scapegoating and feeling shame can slip into bullying. My focus is on recognising that the capacity to slip into bullying behaviour is within each of us. There is good material to help us begin to respond to especially difficult people, but I encourage us to start with the ordinary behaviours that any of us may fall into. I see the potential to bully as being within every member of a congregation and every minister.

The philosopher and anthropologist René Girard's scapegoating theory[1] has its roots in both classical literature and Christian scripture. He identifies a pattern of behaviour where we seek to release individual or community tensions by making a sacrifice in times of trouble. I identify this with bullying. He roots scapegoating in competition between people who are similar to each other. He offers the challenge to Christians to learn, from the cross, that we must give up the attempt to sacrifice others to make ourselves feel better. I believe a major barrier to addressing bullying is that Christian people often do not recognise when they are creating a scapegoat in response to individual or community tensions. If a bullied person leaves a congregation, bystanders and bullies alike may feel a sense of catharsis. There may be the language of death and resurrection with hope for the future. The painful aspect of this is the temporary nature of the sense of release; the behaviour will most likely be repeated when tensions build up again. The underlying problem of bullying may never be identified. This barrier to addressing bullying consists in not seeing the wrongness of bullying and more than that, construing it positively.

I came to Girard's work as a vicar within the Church of England researching bullying as part of doctoral study. It was my own early ministerial experiences which led to an interest in this area. In my work I surveyed the clergy of a diocese regarding how often they experienced behaviours that could contribute to bullying and invited anyone who wanted, to meet and speak with me. This work suggested on a statistical level that some 10 per cent of clergy may be experiencing severe bullying. In practice, this had an outworking in the clergy I surveyed leaving posts to minister in new dioceses, retire, or when employment ended, to seek redress. I did not encounter any clergy who resolved a bullying situation and continued in the place where the problem had occurred. There is a real risk in speaking out, in an already painful situation. Is a target of bullying prepared to risk losing what they have in the hope of resolving the bullying situation? By the time the answer is yes, it is likely too late to have a chance of a positive outcome. A significant barrier to addressing bullying is the approach of waiting for the target of bullying to come forward and make a complaint.

If we consider competition to be the root of scapegoating behaviour, then perhaps we can recognise the significance of an early sense in bystanders that people are treading on each other's toes. This might be over how to set up for a service, or who gets their way at a church council meeting. It might be the power to influence worship in particular directions, or to draw people to a particular project. The church is at risk if it simply allows these small points of conflict to simmer. This is not a matter of being tolerant and allowing for human foibles, it is creating the environment in which conflict can shift into bullying. If we give time to reaching agreement about how things are done in church, being clear about roles and responsibilities, helping people know how they can be heard if they want to bring change, then we are reducing the risk of bullying. This points us to our attitudes and skills; most people have some ability to sort out small disagreements, so let's do more of that. Equally, we all have more to learn. How many Christians have undertaken the very well established Bridgebuilders training to get greater insight into responding to conflict? How many church councils have used material from their denomination to explore their role together? My guess is that the answer to these questions is: not enough! Barriers to addressing bullying relating to conflict are naïvety about the risk of small conflicts, underusing existing abilities to work together, and resistance to further learning.

An additional risk is that the church may be particularly vulnerable to competitive, conflict-driven scapegoating because of the centrality of role models in ministry and faith development. In the Old Testament think of Elijah and Elisha, teacher and apprentice. In the

New Testament, Paul offers many invitations for people to be like him in practising their faith. There can be great value in this apprentice approach to faith development and ministry training, but it risks the apprentice and experienced person becoming too much alike, working too closely together. They may then lack the clear boundaries and distinctiveness of vocation that would lead to them drawing on more varied resources. A quite subtle barrier to addressing bullying may be that we expect similar people to work well together when it might, more rightly, be a concern to be managed through giving space and boundaries or avoided by promoting greater diversity.

Perhaps you are noticing that many of the barriers I am mentioning seem relatively easy to address with normal healthy ways of working together. This leads to a question of why so many Christian people and congregations do not see, do not know, or do not understand such a significant problem. A difficult but important thing to consider is that a person or organisation ignoring bullying is receiving some sort of gain.[2] This could be a social or material gain through someone not rocking the boat, or the catharsis I mentioned earlier. However, a darker gain for an organisation is that a target of bullying may well work harder, work longer, hold off on taking sick leave, and generally pour themselves into their ministry in an attempt to be beyond reproach. A church leadership gaining through bullying is in the territory of serious sin whether they understand what they are doing or not.

There is another strand within human nature that comes to mind when people are ignoring problems. This is the role of our sensitivity to shame when choosing our actions and responses. Stephen Pattison describes a double blindness to things we consider shameful. Those who are ashamed of something feel the need to hide that experience. When what is shameful becomes visible, those around them try not to see what is happening. This brings to mind an interview with a minister who spoke as a bystander to a bullying episode. Upon reflection they thought their colleague was bullied by both senior leadership and congregation members. However, they had not spoken about this with their colleague because they considered that they had a good relationship with them and did not want to spoil it. There is a sense in which the colleague might be embarrassed to know that being a target of bullying was apparent to others. It was not a surprise to me that the colleague has since retired. This brings together some of the more subtle barriers of responding to bullying. Shame and gain working together; we might have imagined that the gain for a bystander remaining silent related to preserving their relationship with a perpetrator of bullying and yet here it is to preserve the relationship with the target of bullying.

Pattison takes the effects of shame a step further[3] when he considers that there are people who have a chronic relationship with shame. He describes the shame-rage spiral as having two sides. A chronically shamed person may attempt to gain a sense of self-worth by identifying with a higher cause in a way that can seem very positive, but they may also bully, manipulate, and intimidate. This offers the understanding that someone who bullies in one context may well, in another, have almost saintly qualities. How many targets of bullying have kept quiet because they know the person doing this is regarded as a saint? Pattison suggests the church is both attractive to chronically shamed people and unlikely to help them address the problem. For Pattison the church is more comfortable operating through the language of guilt than shame. He describes guilt as working around ideas of offence, debt, and punishment, while shame relates to defilement, pollution, and stain. Do our difficulties in responding to bullying have their foundation in our inability to address shame? Sometimes there can be a desire to label a person as a bully. This can be problematic because we may misinterpret the behaviour of a target of bullying as they reach breaking point, but also because to try and manage a chronically shamed person through more shame is unlikely to be constructive.

If we bring scapegoating and shame together, I believe we arrive at another barrier to addressing bullying, that of blame. Where many people and many conflicts come together, blame can land on one person, who may be surprised to discover they are the scapegoat. It is not that the scapegoat has any particular set of personality traits, simply that the blame had to go somewhere. This connection between scapegoating and blame is also picked up by the theologian James Alison,[4] who describes the problem of us blaming Adam and Eve for their sin rather than thanking them for showing us how much we need God. If we find ourselves focusing on blaming someone or agreeing as a bystander that someone is to blame, then we are contributing to the risk of bullying.

I hope that I have illustrated examples of two types of barriers to addressing bullying in the church. Firstly, the scapegoating response to tensions that can lead any of us into bullying behaviour; and secondly, the shame response that generates bullying behaviour in some, and leads both bystanders and targets towards silence. I would like to encourage all of us to begin to address these with our own behaviour towards others. As potential sources of bullying behaviour, let's ask ourselves hard questions about our challenging relationships: What is motivating us? Can we bring change as we are or do we need to develop our skills? As bystanders are we prepared to give time to resolving small conflicts? Do we express concern for targets of bullying and disapproval of bullying behaviour?

These questions may seem a very small starting point compared to a very big problem but if we are unwilling to start with ourselves, then how can we speak to others?

---

[1]   Girard, René, *I See Satan Fall Like Lightning* (New York: Orbis, 2001).

[2]   Beale, D., and Hoel, H., 2011, 'Workplace Bullying and the Employment Relationship: Exploring Questions of Prevention, Control and Context', *Work, Employment and Society* [e-journal] 25(1), pp. 5-18.

[3]   Pattison, S., *Shame, Theory, Therapy, Theology* (Cambridge: Cambridge University Press, 2000).

[4]   Alison, J., *The Joy of Being Wrong, Original Sin Through Easter Eyes* (New York: The Crossroad Publishing Company, 1998).

12

Why Do People Find it Difficult to Grasp the Nettle of Bullying?

ANNE LEE

R esearch has shown that there are a number of factors which make it difficult to understand and accept that bullying happens within churches: belief in a just world, moral disengagement, DARVO (Deny, Attack, Reverse Victim and Offender), and secrecy, as well as the baseline view that Christians love each other so would not, could not, bully or be abusive to each other in any way. All these responses make the person who made the response into an enabler. They are enabling the bullying to continue by refusing to believe it is happening, or by blaming the target and saying it is their fault they are being bullied. Saying nothing is functionally equivalent to condoning bullying behaviour. Saying nothing is frequently the catalyst which turns somebody who should be a supporter of a target into an enabler.

Belief in a Just World

Melvin Lerner's Just World Hypothesis was originally formulated to describe a particular state of cognitive dissonance, a state which occurs in situations involving a violation of justice. The belief that the world is just enables the individual to confront his physical and social environments as though they were stable and orderly. Good things happen to good people and bad things happen to bad people.

A belief in a fundamentally fair world is a comfort. It's a way of maintaining the vital illusion that we, the healthy and prosperous, are not just fortunate, but also somehow deserving. This attitude has penetrated the churches and made it even more difficult for targets of abuse to report their abuse. The view is that if they are being abused, it must in some way be their own fault.

Moral disengagement

Moral disengagement is the separation of moral standards from moral behaviour to permit immoral conduct. Bullying behaviour is immoral because it humiliates and oppresses the targets and can have far-reaching consequences for the physical and psychological health of the target, their friends and families, as well as the organisations in which they work. If people are aware of bullying either as bystanders or as pastoral carers, it is equally immoral if they do nothing about it.

Moral disengagement is the process of convincing oneself that normal ethical standards do not apply in a particular context. It results in the perpetration of inhumanities through moral justification. Do people bully because they lack moral competence, the knowledge of right and wrong, or because they lack an emotional awareness or conscience when it comes to moral transgressions? Bishops who do nothing when faced with evidence of bullying behaviours are disengaging from their understanding of morality. It is moral disengagement when bishops do not act when they know a particular cleric is sexually abusing children or adults. It is moral disengagement when bullying is trivialised as 'banter' or 'teasing' or 'a personality clash'. It is moral disengagement which allows known abuse to continue without calling the abuser to account.[1]

Albert Bandura suggested that there are eight mechanisms which are used to justify immoral behaviour:

1.   Moral justification
2.   Euphemistic labelling
3.   Advantageous comparison
4.   The disregard or distortion of consequences
5.   Displacement of responsibility
6.   Diffusion of responsibility
7.   Dehumanisation
8.   Attribution of blame.

DARVO

DARVO is a response perpetrators of wrongdoing often make when confronted with their behaviour. The acronym was put forward by Jennifer Freyd in her work looking at sexual abuse. DARVO stands for: Deny, Attack, Reverse the roles of Victim and Offender. DARVO is not only an individual response, it can also be an institutional one. Institutional DARVO can be seen in the response of churches and Christian organisations to allegations of sexual wrongdoing by clergy. DARVO is also a common response by perpetrators of bullying in churches. Comments such as 'I'm not the bully, she is bullying me'; or when an individual has been raped, saying 'she asked for it', or 'what does she expect when she wears clothes like that'. All these are DARVO responses. Offenders frequently make threats and overt and covert attacks on the target's credibility. By denying, attacking, and changing perpetrators into victims, reality becomes very confusing and unsafe for the target, the real victim. 'If the victim does speak out and gets this level of attack, she quickly gets the idea that silence is safer.' This strategy is also outlined in the Church of England Ministry Division's 2008 Report, *Dignity at Work*:

> Bullies normally adopt a threefold strategy of defence: (i) Denial, (ii) Counter attack against the complainant and (iii) 'Poor me' thereby gaining sympathy and potentially avoiding the penalty of their behaviour, in effect presenting themselves as the 'victim' and the target as the bully.

Secrecy

There is often a faulty understanding when discerning the difference between secrecy and confidentiality. Confidentiality is extremely important, but we need to understand when it is necessary and appropriate. Secrecy can be abusive and frequently protects perpetrators. 'We knew what was happening, but we thought we had better keep quiet about it.' Too many churches and other religious groups, as well as other employers, have relied on Non-disclosure Agreements (NDAs) to silence targets of a variety of abuses. A press release from the UK government on 8 July 2025 announced that the new 'Employment Rights Bill will ban employers from using non-disclosure agreements that silence workplace harassment and abuse'.[2] To clarify, the aim of the bill is to ban employers from imposing NDAs to silence those complaining about workplace harassment and abuse.

As can be seen in a number of chapters in this book, targets of bullying and other abuse often report that there has been deafening silence from those in senior positions of the church who the targets had thought were there in pastoral roles, to help them. Silence is being weaponised here. Targets who have sent an email to, for example, a bishop they assume to be in both a leadership and a pastoral role for them, report they get the automated response: 'email deleted and not read.' An archdeacon in a speech to General Synod in July 2010 said, 'As an archdeacon I do everything I can to protect the resources of the church at whatever level I am working at.' 'Protecting the resources' of the church was clearly more important to him than listening to a target of bullying and dealing with the bullying which had been disclosed.

Dignity at Work (2008)

This report was the first attempt by the Deployment, Remuneration, and Conditions of Service Committee (DRACSC) of the Church of England to address the topic of bullying in the Church; it included suggested policies and procedures. Copies were sent to all diocesan secretaries who were asked to distribute it around their dioceses. Church of England dioceses are autonomous, so it was not possible to require them to use the report. The report had two major errors in it. The chair of DRACSC at that time insisted that: 1) bullying is rare, and 2) the first thing a target should do was initiate a discussion with the perpetrator. By saying that bullying is rare, he was making it even more difficult for anybody to disclose their abuse. Victims and survivors of abuse frequently take years before they are able to report it. Even though he was presented with evidence that bullying is common in churches, he insisted *Dignity at Work* should say that it is rare.

Should the target of bullying speak to the perpetrator to try to get it stopped? Research has for many years shown that having a meeting between the target and the perpetrator will escalate the abuse and make it much worse. People in the church often go to the Bible to justify their actions. Matthew 18:15 says, 'If another member of the church sins against you, go and point out the fault when the two of you are alone. If the member listens to you, you have regained that one'.

The word 'sin' in Matthew 18 is not the same as 'abuse'. It does not say, 'If another member of the church abuses you …'. To encourage someone who is being abused to go to speak to the person who is abusing them, is to reinforce and create further abuse. In one diocese when a target was asked to go to her perpetrator, she said, 'Being asked to go to talk to my perpetrator is like being asked to be in the same room as my rapist.'

Future needs

Far more research needs to be done, especially in the UK, to determine the antecedents, consequences, and prevalence of bullying in Christian churches and parachurch organisations. Research is also needed to determine what would be optimal in the theological education institutions and in the training of bishops and archdeacons to help clergy identify and deal appropriately and positively with conflict and bullying. A day course, 'Combatting and Dealing with Difficult Behaviour', was devised in 2010 for current and new bishops in the Church of England. The aims of the day were:

- To raise awareness of harassment and bullying and the forms this behaviour takes.
- With reference to the framework offered in the *Dignity at Work* booklet, to facilitate a greater understanding of the Church of England's legal responsibilities.
- To better enable bishops to put the harassment and bullying policy into practice to promote a harassment-free environment.
- To examine and practise skills appropriate for dealing with a range of difficult situations.

Unfortunately no bishops applied to go on the course. It was then opened to all senior staff in all dioceses. Nobody applied. The course was cancelled. It has not been offered again.

There is also a need to locate research in the language of theology to help clergy and senior denominational staff understand the issues, the complexities surrounding bullying, and the necessity of dealing decisively with bullying and harassment. Stephen Finlan, a pastor with the United Church of Christ, has looked at the theology of bullying from a North American perspective; Pete Myers and Selina Stone in the UK have also written on the subject, but much more needs to be done. This has begun to happen when exploring sexual abuse in churches. There are also a number of theological resources looking at the abuse of power (see bibliography). However, there is still a need to back up the large amount of anecdotal evidence of bullying within churches with serious, peer-reviewed research.

---

[1]   Lovett, Jo, Coy, Maddy, and Kelly, Liz, *Deflection, denial and disbelief: social and political discourses about child sexual abuse and their influence on institutional responses. A rapid evidence assessment* (London: IICSA/London Metropolitan University, 2018). https://www.iicsa.org.uk/reports-recommendations/publications/research/social-political-discourses.html

[2]   https://www.gov.uk/government/news/ban-on-controversial-ndas-silencing-abuse Accessed 15 November 2025

13

Bullying, Power and Hierarchy

JOY ALLAN

Introduction: A personal account

As a teenager I was, perhaps unsurprisingly, bullied. A girl with a squint, a big house, a Christian faith, and a penchant for books (and words like 'penchant'); high school was always going to be tricky. Especially so when that high school was the home of war and rumours of war: 'hair-fires', 'head-flushings', blood flowing down corridors after not infrequent fights, and individuals such as 'Bob', who took it upon themselves to remind the 'squinty-eyed' girl of her place in the school pecking order.

I am grateful that, unlike others, my bullying was limited to 'emotional' abuse. Yet we know that even emotional and psychological bullying leaves its scars, some say even deeper and longer lasting than 'mere' physical assault. That I escaped relatively unscathed I put down to the Christian community which came into my life around the same time as the bullies. This very quickly became my home and my refuge.

Perhaps inevitably, some years later that 'home', or at least some factions of it, became a source of something more akin to hate than hearth. I did not fare well. How could I? My refuge had turned into my ruin. That ruin ripped across my life, tearing a hole in family relations, friendships, and ultimately my own mental health. It is only in the past few years that I have crawled out of that ruin and have realised the crucible it has become for my theological thinking and work, even when it did not consciously inform it.

Spending my life around church leaders and theologians as I do, I am aware that I am far from alone in this experience. All too frequently, I hear heart-breaking stories of spiritual abuse, bullying, manipulation, and cowardice in the Church. If it were not for a God who seems to keep pursuing me, it would be enough to break me; at times it has come close.

I am forced to ask: is this the story we wish to tell? Theologically, how do we turn to the one by whose scars we are healed? Evangelistically, how do we live out a faith in the Christ whose mission seems to have been not to the powerful but to the meek, the weak, and the lowly? How do we live lives which will call back those who have been so hurt they have left our fold? Pastorally, how do we care well for those who have been significantly traumatised by bullying?

This is not just an issue which affects the perpetrators and their targets; it is one which reaches deep into the root of both *who* we are and *whose* we are. It shines a light on our idolatry and complicity. Consideration of it, then, teaches us fundamental truths about the movements of which we are part.

It is important in saying this, to specify the community of which I am part, and thus my potential bias. My upbringing, training, career and (alas) painful experiences have taken place within the broader sphere of evangelicalism. Nonetheless, I am convinced that what I am about to write is applicable to all Christians, for the following reasons:

1. The reach and growth of evangelicalism is widely documented. Even if one's church is not evangelical the influence of such entities as CCM, evangelical youth movements, and Christian media means it is unlikely many churches are left untouched, even in subtle and often unconscious ways (e.g. the theology in the songs we sing).
2. Even if this were not the case, my time in other denominations and my reading of the literature has shown that (sadly) the issue of bullying is all too prevalent in all of our churches.

So let us consider that issue and our response to it. In order to do so it is imperative that we consider two matters which are core not only to the struggle of bullying but to the church: power and relationship.

Power and relationship: two components of bullying

As is frequently stated, there is (perhaps surprisingly) no legal definition of bullying; although Northern Ireland does have a legal definition of bullying as it applies in schools. However, a quick glance across general definitions demonstrates the centrality of these two concepts.

In agreement with diverse sources, the Anti-Bullying Alliance defines bullying as the '… intentional hurting of one person or group by another person or group, where the relationship involves an imbalance of power'. There is a fine line between bullying and spiritual/emotional abuse: coercive control, power, and manipulation are, unfortunately, key aspects in each of these areas. The Church is not currently best placed to respond to these aspects. In fact, it is all too frequently a hothouse in which they can grow. It is important that we turn to considering why that might be and what we should do about it.

Power and relationship: current Christian responses?

I have spent much of the years since finishing my PhD teaching a range of subjects within theology. I have been consistently saddened and surprised at the sheer ubiquity with which, across this range of subjects – doctrinal debates, issues in pastoral care, theology in the public sphere, and within the Church herself – the power we have (or don't have) and the ways in which we wield it over one another are all too easily evident.

A book which I have appreciated greatly in both its bravery and its diagnosis of this, is *Jesus and John Wayne* by Kristin Kobes Du Mez. Beginning with Trump's assertions of power and Christendom's apparent desire for it, Du Mez questions if this is an anomaly or rather, 'the culmination of evangelicals' embrace of militant masculinity, an ideology that enshrines patriarchal authority and condones the callous display of power, at home and abroad'.[1] This point is consistently made throughout the work, with reference to many movements and names that will be familiar to us.

Whether we agree or disagree with her thesis, the material within this work should at least unsettle those of us within the pews (or plastic seats!) of evangelicalism. Given the relative fame and far-reaching nature of the names and ministries mentioned, it should unsettle us all.

Closer to home, this has been made further evident by the work of disability theologians who remind us that theology which is not applicable to the lives of those we see as 'weak' or 'dependent' is quite simply not good theology. Much of such theology pervades our churches and is achingly evident in our practices. We must ask, how much of our numbers-driven evangelism, image-driven 'success' in the public sphere, and declarations from the pulpit or stage are applicable to those we see as weak?

All too often they are not applicable. We enter the Christian world as I did, thinking it a refuge, unaware of the machinations that are going on beneath the 'kind' words of PCCs, standing committees, and leadership bids. This book will have shown not only the pervasiveness of this, but the scars which it can inflict.

This is particularly the case because of the *hidden* nature of the influence of power and relationship within the Church. Firstly, this is due to the ways in which bullying often occurs in churches. The true dynamics of power are not often visible. Those who have power are often those who have the loudest voices, the most authoritative ministries, the vicar or pastor's ear, or the most evident gifts. This is particularly difficult when those people become the perpetrators of bullying, as they have been put in that position precisely due to their 'godliness'. Who are we to question that godliness? The victims all too often turn inwards, questioning whether bullying even occurred, mitigating the disaster that has been borne upon them, until it is too late; the scars are already weeping.

Sadly, there are hiddenness and scars not only in the prevalence and places of power in our churches, but in the ways in which we relate to one another. If we consider, for example, our own faith stories, we will most likely utter phrases such as 'I first saw X live a different kind of life ...'; 'it was Y who told me about Jesus...'; or, 'Z told me about church'. We come to faith in a nexus of relationships. Yet, all too often when we run into significant problems, we are simply told 'this is between you and God, you must sort this out'.[2]

This can be seen with a glance at the literature in our Christian bookshops, or in the hands of well-meaning friends supporting those dealing with bullying and emotional abuse. It shocks me how often Christian books start not with an aching with the victim, but with the question of how the victim can cease attracting bullies, can work on their own faith, and can heal by gathering more resilience.

Yet resilience isn't gained by simply willing it. It is gained in community. It is gained in the surrounding love of others healing our scars, pouring out the ointment of praise – praise that silences the inner critic born of the bully. Speaking love where hate was uttered, peace where war was fought, and building up the nexus of relationships in which faith was first born.

Resilience is also found in lament. As Christians, we say that we stand in the same scriptures that incorporate the psalms of lament, the book of Lamentations, Job, and the tears of the prophets. We say we stand in the scriptures and the Spirit of Christ: the God who mourned Lazarus knowing he would raise him; who walked the Emmaus road *with* the disciples, allowing them to declare him dead, after he was raised.

Yet, do we allow those who are broken to *be* broken, or do we chivvy them on, terrified that they will speak sadness, heresy, something which may be distasteful to God or (more likely) to us? It seems to me (from both my experience and research) we would be more likely to turn the lamentations to a major chord, run to awaken Lazarus, and tell the disciples on the Emmaus road that they were mistaken.

There are of course reasons for this. It is important that we examine ourselves, attract the good, resist the bad, and have the discernment to know the difference. The problem is that not many people I have cared for (nor indeed I myself) were ready to do that work *until we had healed at least a little.* In fact, in rushing this process, all that tends to be gained is more hurt, anger, and inactivity.

My suggestion is a deceptively simple one, and as such I give it tentatively, knowing the complexity of this issue: be like Christ.

The disciples were not ready to know him, so he walked with them (Luke 24:13-35).

The people were mourning, so he mourned with them (John 11).

They, and we, were not ready for a messiah who would come in the lineage of Rahab the questionable, Ruth the 'other', and David the smallest. So, he came anyway. On a donkey no less.

He took our idolatry and showed us what power really looked like. Why then are we still clamouring after our kind of power? Preaching against 'the world' when all too often it lives within us, our systems, our choices, our hagiography? It would seem that the saints of the scriptures are quite different to those whom we may choose.

So here is my simple (yet complex) suggestion. Let us mourn, let us resist, let us love one another, let us walk, let us run. And may that running be hard and fast, into the arms of he whose kingdom consists not of kings but of the weak, the meek, the outcast and even, perhaps, the squinty-eyed theologian. For of such is (thankfully!) the kingdom of heaven.

---

[1]   Du Mez, Kristin Kobes, *Jesus and John Wayne – How White Evangelicals Corrupted a Faith and Fractured a Nation* (Liveright Kindle edition), p. 3.

[2]   I explore this in greater detail in my PhD thesis, which is freely available at: Allan, Deborah Joy, 'Sertraline,

Suffering, and the Spirit: How Do Pentecostal/Charismatic Christians Respond Faithfully to Depression?', University of Aberdeen, 2018. https://abdn.alma.exlibrisgroup.com/discovery/delivery/44ABE_INST:44ABE_VU1/12152504340005941

14

Bullying and its Enablers

DEIRDRE GOOD

Not long ago I stood at the front of a Methodist church in North Carolina, preparing to read at a joint worship service of Methodists and Episcopalians. It was late afternoon in a southern climate, and the warm sun shone in through the translucent blue stained-glass windows. The space was open and light. As I stood whispering the words of Jesus' farewell in the text of John's gospel, 'My peace I leave with you ... Peace I leave with you; my peace I give to you. I do not give to you as the world gives. Do not let your hearts be troubled, and do not let them be afraid' (John 14:27-28 (NIV)), I could hear members of the group behind me moving into the worship space quietly to sit in pews. While I knew no one well, we had just spent several days together in conversation living into the exciting possibility of shared Methodist and Episcopal worship after decades of conversation. I was optimistic about the process and possibility of unity, and felt as I stood there, bonds of affection in the experience of dialogue. We had shared Eucharist.

But I could feel at the same time in my body an anxiety, a tension. What was it? Was it nervousness before reading a familiar text out loud? Or something else? As I paused, lost in thought, suddenly into my head came these words: 'Whatever anxiety you feel now is nothing compared to the anxiety you felt at the seminary back then.' My body relaxed slowly in this new space as my mind went back immediately to the chapel of the seminary where I had worshipped for twenty-eight years. On the day I was remembering, a day in the last year I was there, I found myself sitting in a pew close to the front of the chapel not praying or meditating, or looking at the stained glass, but unconsciously eyeing exit routes. I caught myself in the present, and asked: escape routes from chapel? What was going on? And it came back to me: I became gradually conscious – as I sat in chapel – that I was mentally planning an escape route to flee from a potential threat coming in either from the west door up through the chapel, or from the side sacristy door and down from the altar at the east end. I was looking for an escape not from something but rather from someone: an ecclesiastical authority figure bearing down on me to compel an exchange of peace where there was no peace. There was no peace: neither inside nor outside chapel, nor in daily meetings, nor in classrooms, nor in dining rooms. Instead, there was the chaos and instability where oppression thrives, and the coercion of peace reflecting the bullying behaviour and influence the perpetrator had on the entire seminary community. Regular chapel was required, several times daily. Instead of a place of peaceful corporate worship, it became a threatening experience of toxic, traumatic terror.

The body knows what the mind comes to recognise and acknowledge. It was involuntarily in my body that I remembered this ordeal of seminary chapel life over a year later. Through somatic knowing I came to understand that no worry I'd felt since then, whether in a journey from a tenured position to abrupt unemployment; or moving house and home after twenty-eight years; or taking a new job in a new location; compared in any way, shape, or form to the trauma not just of chapel worship but of daily life at the seminary. And in the safe space of a North Carolina Methodist church over a year later I could remember this first in my body and, by reliving some of the danger I felt in a faraway safe place, to continue to heal.

My traumatic memory of events during regular worship in a seminary chapel included experiences overshadowing what should have been a sharing of the peace amongst congregants, with the sense of being subjugated even in a new place of worship where I knew intellectually there was only good will.

In an essay on enablers of bullies and bullying, I start with a description of trauma resulting from an experience of being bullied during worship to remind readers that enablers enable and effectuate not only bullies and bullying, but all the accompanying and subsequent embodied trauma suffered by their victims both during the experience and for years afterwards. Worshippers expect to worship God in a safe haven. They do not expect worship leaders to coerce participants into actions during the service that convey the opposite religious meaning from the one intended. And by extension, enablers who appoint such worship leaders without adequate safeguards, be they senior administrators or members of governing bodies, are not passive bystanders but actively complicit in the intimidation taking place, and its traumatic effects.

At the seminary they deliberately avoided the harm that was being done, because at that point they knew that accusations of intimidation and harm had been made. Yet even with knowledge of these accusations, they did nothing to inhibit such actions. Charged with a duty of care for community well-being, and with direct knowledge of bullying and danger, they forsook their responsibility of oversight and care for the community and fled, leaving students, staff, visitors, and faculty deserted and vulnerable to coercive acts by an ostensible leader in unsafe places of community gatherings.

Such enablers act only to protect institutions and their leaders at the expense of victims. Moreover, those who experienced such bullying also experienced, at the core of their being, a violation of trust and abandonment at the hands of trustees and leaders in an institution to which their pastoral leaders, their priests and bishops back home, had entrusted them. People were harmed in the very place in which they were being formed as spiritual leaders and priests; and by the very people held up as model spiritual guides whose leadership, enabled by the silence of governors, trustees, and senior staff, sought to compel touch and thereby mar and injure bodies, souls, and spirits. The very hands that consecrated bread also mandated oppression.

Many factors contribute to workplace bullying including enabling, motivating, and precipitating. The literature shows that human resource management can offer a number of practical solutions to tackle these antecedents to bullying. Enablers enable structures and processes that make it possible for bullying to occur in the first place. These structures can be work-specific or organisational. Work-related enabling factors include role ambiguity and conflict; excessive, unreasonable, and unexpected last-minute job demands, and limited or no job autonomy. Organisational enablers facilitate a normalised bullying culture by failing to provide support for identification of bullying and its prevention, thus enabling management initiatives and leadership styles that are typically more authoritarian. The antidote is a thorough job analysis with well-defined, well-communicated job roles and a strong review process, both essential to tackle enabling work factors. The support of organisational leaders, board, and management from the outset for all parties is critical for any prevention initiative. Boundaries and expectations that are established and led from the top, coupled with strengthening the socialisation process and onboarding of new hires, help to destabilise and even prevent an emergence of bullying. Training in performance management and delivery feedback, together with identification and awareness of bullying, in addition to management-led anti-bullying policies help develop leaders who recognise a need for safeguards and who monitor and enact change.

Motivating factors – that is, particular circumstances and systems within an organisation which might indirectly encourage or incentivise bullying behaviours – may be identified in a workplace. Insularity from best practices in, for example, hiring procedures may lead organisations to look only in specific and restricted pools for new hiring, based on a restricted world view, and limited accountability. Years ago, I was one of three finalists for a junior position. I learned later that the search committee had placed me in the top position but that the academic dean had reversed the placement and put me last on the grounds that I, as a foreign national, was completely unknown, and would be unfamiliar with the ethos of the institution. Hiring me would involve completing additional paperwork to help me to procure a visa. In the event I was hired for the job due to outside factors: the other two candidates secured positions elsewhere. In another case, as head of the search committee for an administrative position, I was advised to eliminate the committee's first choice (after months of work) on the grounds that our well-qualified candidate would be too expensive in a not-for-profit institution. In my compliance, I was forced to be complicit in a (typical?) process established by senior administration undermining best practices. But well planned and public hiring practices demonstrate accountability to hiring norms and transparency, thus counteracting a smaller, dangerously insular world view, with its wasted energies, dishonesties, and deceit alongside enabling.

Precipitating contributions to bullying not identified or corrected by senior administration would include extensive use of part-time or temporary workers or pay cuts, together with a failure to conduct transparent assessment regularly. Policies emphasising permanent employment and tenure, strengthening the socialisation and onboarding programme for full and part-time workers, ensure that staff understand institutional culture and ways to, for example, identify and deal with bullying. Unannounced freezes to promotions, and sudden changes in organisational management or restructures can trigger workplace bullying. At times of change and high pressure, human resources personnel need to support staff by ensuring they manage conflicts that may arise. In such times of stress, bullying is more likely to occur.

To know about bullying misconduct and abuse is to be a party to it. At issue is what the enablers do with that knowledge. If those who know of bullying behaviour are silent or passive, they are complicit in enabling, endorsing, and thus permitting continuation of bullying conduct, and concomitant trauma for targets. Why and for what reasons do enablers refuse to act, leaving victims vulnerable to further terrors? Some motives have a particular resonance with the language and thought worlds of religious institutions and churches, while others are shared with more general situations of abuse.

Among the former reasons are deference to persons with institutional and religious authority: presidents, deans, bishops, and clergy members of governing boards or faculties; who are presumed to hold the safety and wellbeing of their churches, seminaries, faculty, staff, and students as their highest priority. In such cases, bully and enabler exist hand in hand, since a bully benefits from the complicity of enablers. From the survivor's perspective, both perpetrator and enablers bear responsibility for their terrible plight and must be held accountable. To use religious language, survivors confront two distinct categories of evil: bully (predator) and enabler. Perpetrators are known and trusted by the community. They are also protected and supported by enablers. Equally culpable is the bystander who sees a victim in the path of the perpetrator, who is capable of action and has the means to act, but who nevertheless decides not to. To date, only the bully or predator has any chance of being held accountable through, for example, criminal prosecution. Enablers may well practise inertia and disbelieve reports of misconduct. Not only are they likely to protect the perpetrator, e.g. by blaming the target, they may also declare allegiance to the institution over the individual who is harmed, and in so doing they desert and abandon the victim who trusted them both.

Enablers make excuses to avoid culpability: I was not there when it happened; I am not a first-hand witness; I do not have direct evidence of the alleged assault; I have a higher duty to the institution than to its particular members - churches, schools, and other ecclesiastical institutions are accountable to a higher authority than those of the secular world. But, let's be clear, enablers who fail to respond to targets of bullying are no less culpable than the bully, even though the human toll of hearing about human pain is something a person might prefer to avoid. Yet, from the victim's point of view, the experience of being ignored after reporting abuse is as painful as the original experience as a target of bullying. In fact, being dismissed or ignored actually re-traumatises the survivor.

In conclusion: the voices of survivors must be prioritised over the survival of an organisation, and ways to hold enablers accountable for their complicity in knowing about and enabling abuse, but not preventing it, must be explored within the criminal justice system.

15

The Post Office at Prayer

MARTYN PERCY

Generally speaking, the British people love their institutions. According to one recent poll, the National Health Service is the most trusted. It won't surprise many to know that major banks, corporations, and political parties are at the other end of the league table, scoring low on trust and respect. What might come as something of a shock is to discover the Church of England and the Post Office hovering precariously in the relegation zone. How is it that two such great and venerable institutions should find themselves in this position?

Of course, it depends which bit of the Post Office or the Church of England one is referring to. Local churches, like local post offices, are usually cherished and well-supported by their communities, especially in rural areas. The sub-postmaster, or postmistress provides an integral service to the local community. Lose the post office, and people will often complain that the heart has been ripped out of the community. It is hardly different with local clergy and churches.

Some years ago, Archbishop Rowan Williams appeared on BBC Radio 4's *Desert Island Discs*. One of the tracks he chose for his virtual exile was the low, warm sound of villagers chatting in the queue at a local Welsh Post Office. One might go further here, and say that the low, warm sound of a cuppa with the congregation after a service is akin to the post office at prayer. There is a sacred quality in being together, gathering our news, being kind to one another, and waiting.

The mistrust in the Post Office and the Church of England is not at this highly-cherished local level. The grim poll that sees these two venerable institutions performing so badly refers to the executives, CEOs, and church leaders. It is these folk, alas, who are mistrusted, not believed, and whose words and assurances are suspected of being disingenuous – or even outright fibs and lies. How did we arrive at this situation? In what ways do these institutions perpetrate abuses, including bullying, neglect, and even cruelty? What of the lack of basic rights for their employees? How do they fare, set against the most basic Nolan Principles for Conduct in Public Life: selflessness, integrity, objectivity, accountability, openness, honesty, and leadership?

Many British people are quietly proud of the fact that the United Kingdom has no written constitution. On the face of it, this presumes that common law and human rights are so obvious to the British that they do not need spelling out. There has been no slavery in England for over 1,000 years, after all. Everybody has access to education, healthcare, and social services. So what could a written constitution add, given that these universals had already been granted?

The lack of a written constitution does prompt a certain degree of national naivety and smugness, but the nineteenth, twentieth and twenty-first centuries tested such presumptions. Are all citizens given equal rights, e.g., on the basis of class, ethnicity, dis-ability, gender, or sexuality? It has taken a while, as movements for universal suffrage had to toil for hundreds of years to overturn the assumption that only property-owning males could vote in parliamentary elections. The legislation to end discrimination in the workplace and in civic life is relatively recent.

There is no doubt that in the past the institution of the British state has been abusive and bullying towards its own people. Just think of the suffragettes, the campaigns to legalise homosexuality, and the more recent Windrush scandal. The British Post Office scandal is currently one of the most serious miscarriages of justice in British legal history. The BBC and ITV dramatisations of the recent Post Office scandals raised some intriguing questions for those who had concerns about other noble institutions at the heart of the British establishment.

Between 1999 and 2015 over 900 sub-post masters, mistresses and officers were prosecuted for theft, false accounting and fraud. In fact, the shortfalls at their branches were entirely due to errors in the Post Office's Fujitsu Horizon accounting software. This was known by senior executives at the Post Office, yet the prosecutions continued, and a comprehensive cover-up was organised to protect the 'brand' of the Post Office.

Had the Church of England rolled out a similar national software package that accounted for the weekly collection in its parish churches, and made all clergy use it, then it is my view that all clergy with any alleged cash shortfalls would have been treated in exactly the same way as the local Post Office and staff. There would have then been several hundred internal church prosecutions led by the Secretariat. The Church of England, like the Post Office, would have been the complainant, investigator, prosecutor, judge, and jury. There would have been no independent fact-finding investigation prior to the defendant being put on trial, and convicted.

No number of suicides, mental health breakdowns, sicknesses, or financially ruined staff would have caused senior church leaders to pause or change course. The lawyers for the Church, much like those for the Post Office, would have been expensive, bullying, aggressive, and obstructive. They would regularly have halted mediation with defendants, and deliberately delayed justice in order to try and break victims. Those accused would have been told that any defence they mounted was likely to increase the prosecution costs, for which defendants would be further liable, and would therefore lead to a harsher sentence once convicted. The Church would have claimed their systems were robust. Defendants – poor clergy with no money – would have been left in despair.

Had there been an Independent Inquiry, the Church of England would have confirmed its main priority was always brand loyalty and reputation management. Senior staff would have argued that clergy were always complaining, with some 'on the take' and 'helping themselves to the collection plate'. The Church, if found culpable in its processes, would have then have offered only a piffling amount of compensation to victims to cover their losses. The Church of England, as the Post Office appears to have done, operates with a guilty-until-proven-innocent outlook. Indeed, the Church of England might be said to be both the modern Tory Party at prayer (hopelessly and viscerally divided on unresolvable issues), and the Post Office at prayer.

The current turn toward ecclesial organisation and management presses the question: is the Church of England a distinctive, bounded, and overtly member-based organisation in character, seeking clarity of identity? Or, is it an institution? I agree that all institutions need some level of organisation. The family unit is the oldest institution in the world; each family will ideally be bound together by values, mutual respect, kindred spirit, and the commitment to cherish, care for, and love one another despite differences. Institutions quickly unravel when such qualities are absent, as the Church of England knows to its cost. However, the relationships in such bodies are rarely contractual, and instead depend on soft forms of power such as goodwill, voluntary support, trust, careful attention, and mindful service.

An Integrity Framework would be a wholly new concept to most English people, but (like the Nolan Principles), the Australian National Audit Office has developed an overarching structure for supporting and managing the integrity of institutions. The Australian Integrity Framework arose out of scandals in policing, military service, government – and was latterly applied to the churches in light of their opacity on sexual abuse cases. The Integrity Framework serves to assist in ethical decision-making and the management of risk, fraud, and misconduct.[1] It handles conflicts of interest, vested interests, whistleblowing, and corruption, as well as the covering up of incompetence and misconduct. Its enduring focus is on promoting integrity as a value embedded in work and culture. It encourages independence, honesty, openness, accountability, and courage.

The Post Office would have failed the tests set out by the Integrity Framework. The Church of England would fail it too, and doubtless seek legal exemption from such a code. Consequently, whistleblowers are not protected, victims are re-abused, abuse is covered up, and the status quo maintained. The result is inevitable. Many doubt that Lambeth Palace, Church House Westminster, bishops and senior clergy, or the CEO and board of the Post Office, have integrity. These bodies seek to remain aloof from scrutiny and accountability. They fear liability and exposure. Their energies are poured into protecting the brand and safeguarding their reputations from damage.

A bi-polarity quickly develops. On the one hand, the Post Office and the Church of England leadership promise to deliver modern corporate step-change management. On the other hand, their leaders behave as monarchs, above any form of accountability or scrutiny, let alone transparency. The Church of England is a monarchical polity, and so only tinkers with cosmetic reform, which is designed to signal modernisation and relevance. The underlying culture of deference and courtiers remains intact, and will always resist external scrutiny, independent regulatory accountability, and even openness.

English Anglicanism can often present itself as authentic and pastorally-grounded in local parishes and chaplaincies. But in its national leadership and structures, the Church of England is often revealed to be a form of aloof polity, rooted in politeness and social hierarchy. This is part of the ecclesial DNA-coding of the Church of England. The more the central governance of the Church tries to invent new initiatives to address its own numerical anxieties and other neuroses, the more the public back away. It also quickly morphs into soft bullying by a demand-led top-down leadership, who simply see clergy and laity as a means to an end: theirs.

That said, pastoral and liturgical aspects of the Church of England continue to be an English collective national treasure. Like Post Offices, and the posties delivering the letters to each door, the local is what matters. Few want a relationship with their remote delivery depot. Likewise for the Church of England, local levels, parish ministry, and chaplaincy continue to be cherished and valued, making appreciable differences to community and civic life. Few want to know about the diocesan headquarters and its strategic vision. As centralisation increases it leads unavoidably into ever-greater disenchantment and disengagement.

The present state of the Church of England would pose an enormous challenge for the very best estate agent to elicit serious interest. True, the Church of England is not for sale; but it is constantly on the lookout for long-term and loyal tenants who will take care of the storefront as though they were the owners. Upkeep, appearance, productivity, regional-brand-compliance, and purpose are devolved to the local occupiers, who mostly do an extremely good job on very tight budgets. For all their labour, laity and clergy will receive little thanks from their somewhat distant landlords, who are only interested in productivity and turnover. They require public compliance too, unless diversification delivers growth. We now have a situation in which the Church of England's senior leadership are re-mortgaging the church on a regular basis. In this, they are banking on the past and borrowing from the future to try and resolve their present issues and crises.

As some may know with their own homes, this is risky – and only makes sense if the value of your property goes up. But as the social, moral, spiritual, and intellectual capital of the Church of England has collapsed into deep negative equity, there is a risk of default at any point. Bridging loans are unlikely to be extended. Local branches may want to start asking some quite basic questions: Who really owns this business? Who does it serve, and for what purposes? Who are these people in regional and national headquarters, telling others how to run things locally, and cutting local support while increasing their own?

Because these rules and codes are not written down – remember, Britain has no written constitution – the elite have extensive interests in maintaining a hierarchical social order that is dependent on class, hereditary power, and the like. English Anglicanism often presents as a kind of spiritualised gentility, a baptism and confirmation of elitism and social hierarchy. A culture rooted in elite white-male, class-based mannered-ness becomes sacralised in ecclesial settings. Mild, slightly aloof, and distant forms of engagement are developed as normative, in order to avoid the difficulty of surfacing competing convictions, and the underlying passions, emotions and desires that are baked in to them. The English, until recently, had a broad appreciation for an ecclesial polity that dovetailed with the normative 'national mood': namely, mildness.

As the Church of England continues to lose its status as a national treasure, and instead becomes an agent in need of membership, support, and sustenance, the identity of the polity shifts from being that of public service to one of community surcharge. The episcopal and ecclesial leadership find themselves unable to resist the temptations of centralised and bureaucratic oversight, including financial control. In turn, that slowly evolving stance depends on demonstrating competence, trust, accountability, transparency, and fairness – and it is at precisely this juncture that the weakness of monarchical models of leadership are at their most exposed. They have few skills for such work.

The lack of an Integrity Framework for the Church of England means that it will continue to engage in bullying behaviours, obfuscate, and evade scrutiny; avoid transparency and accountability; and seek to remain outside normative standards and codes of conduct for public life. The consequences of this will fall upon a never-ending supply of victims seeking justice and reparation. The ultimate end, however, will be the dismantling and death of an institution that was once loved and admired by the public, but can no longer command the trust and respect of its employees and people who once gave their lives to work for it.

---

[1] See https://www.anao.gov.au/work/corporate/anao-integrity-framework-and-report-2022-23: and Miller, Seumas, *The Moral Foundations of Social Institutions* (Cambridge: CUP, 2010); *Organizing Leviathan: Politicians, Bureaucrats, and the Making of Good Government* (Cambridge: CUP, 2017); and on institutional failings, https://www.premierchristianity.com/opinion/uccf-its-time-for-me-to-say-sorry/17095.article.

16

The Empire Strikes Back: The Intersection of Race, Sexuality and Ministry as it Relates to Bullying

AUGUSTINE TANNER-IHM

Many of my generation were brought up with a familiar nursery rhythm: 'Sticks and bones may break my bones, but words will never hurt me.' I think this is the first lie children are told. Not the lie that Father Christmas does not like the North Pole or that he freely gives gifts to those whose good actions outweigh their bad. Or even that there is a magical tiny fairy that gives you money when you dispose of your teeth under your pillow. Arguably these are harmless and just a part of cultural folklore. But this so-called nursery rhyme changes the foundations of psychological development for many people. It teaches us that the words we hear are not very painful. But we all know that words have power. They are often strongholds in our mental and emotional well-being. Hurtful words can be like an overpowering army with military-grade weapons when you're alone, trying to position yourself in some form of safety.

Aggressive words are commonly called microaggressions. Microaggressions are a form of bullying. In a concept propounded by Kevin Nadal, microaggressions are the small, often unnoticed comments or actions – whether deliberate or accidental – that express prejudice or bias toward people from marginalised backgrounds.

As a Black queer Christian working in majority environments that are cis-gender, white, and heteronormative, I have had to continually negotiate questions of perception, belonging, and authenticity in order to function within those spaces. A layered negotiation is required when one's identity intersects multiple marginalised categories within ecclesial and institutional contexts that presume normative whiteness and heterosexuality.

When Black people are assertive and stand up for ourselves our character and competency often come into question. The fear of the angry, aggressive Black man or woman stereotype is often used to scapegoat white people's fears of blackness. It's when you sit in a first-class carriage on a train and the ticket officer doesn't check anyone else's ticket to make sure they're in the correct place but only checks yours, a Black man's. Or your boss commenting on how articulate you are. Or someone touching your hair without asking you, because they wanted to feel how different your hair was.

These experiences of everyday microaggressions could have the effect of creating bitter or isolated persons because they constitute emotional and mental waterboarding. They erode one's sense of self and identity until one eventually breaks. These microaggressions occur because of what scholars call infrahumanisation, which is a tendency for people to perceive individuals in other groups as being somewhat less human.[1]

These acts of infrahumanisation and dehumanisation

can cause serious mental health problems and racial trauma. According to Unison, the UK's biggest union:

> Black women employees are *twice* as likely to be bullied as their white colleagues. For example, 52 per cent of Black Caribbean, 56 per cent of Black Africans, and 51 percent of UK-born Black employees reported being bullied compared to 33 per cent of white employees. This increased to 67 per cent when those in the category 'Black other' was included.[2]

We have seen this in a variety of cases in different industries, but unfortunately also within the Christian Church. The Church of England's Ministry Council commissioned a report by Dr Selina Stone entitled, *'If it Wasn't for God': A Report on the Wellbeing of Global Majority Heritage Clergy in the Church of England*. The report looks at the experiences of non-white clergy and clergy in training and gives shocking examples of how bullying and microaggressions are not limited to the secular world, but are a problem in the church as well. It examines the constant negotiation between one's own culture and the dominant culture around. Often, those who do not assimilate into the mostly white Eurocentric culture are considered trouble, and their career or vocation is in jeopardy. This negatively affects the minister and their family and support network.

Now let's add another very important element, human sexuality: a very difficult conversation to have. But both forms of intersectional microaggressions are happening to many people who are both LGBTQIA and an ethnic minority. If we add gender, disability, neurodiversity, sex, or any other characteristic protected under the 2010 Equality Act, life at work can be made unbearable. This unintentional or intentional bullying has a massive effect on a person's well-being and productivity.

Bullying should have no place in the ministry or wider society because of its moral nature, and the breaking of the understanding that we are all made in the image of God. From an economic flourishing viewpoint, this is not good for productivity. Therefore, several companies and scholars have invested in the theory of psychological safety. Amy Edmondson writes in *The Fearless Organization,* 'psychological safety is a belief that one will not be humiliated or punished for speaking up with ideas, questions, concerns, or mistakes and that the team is safe for interpersonal risk-taking'. This is a radically different way in which we in churches should be functioning. Too often marginalised persons feel unloved and unvalued in teams and places of work because of an aspect of their personhood. This is where psychological safety comes into play. Your ministry or place of work – is this a place where people can be themselves without feeling the weight of cultural assimilation? Within your teams is there good dialogue about different viewpoints and how they contribute to a better outcome?

Does your organisation or company have an inside saying about, 'Play the game?' Playing the game is a way of life. It reflects a culture where the employee or person who desires to be a part of the system in which they are trying to gain a place at the table gets the message: 'you must get rid of your personality and your cultural customs and conform to the majority of people in this organisation. You must learn to code-switch, adapting language, affect, and cultural reference points to align with the dominant vernacular' – as though one's value were contingent on the ability to conform to majority expectations. There is a systemic demand for individuals from marginalised identities to perform an additional layer of cultural translation in order to be considered credible. These are the ways to play the game, the way to gain entry into a system that is against you – while also losing part of yourself.

This is the game of the Empire. The game of the Empire will always be bullying, exclusion, and domination. We are subjects of an emperor, not a benevolent king. An empire is a place of battle and will fight with everything it has to defend its customs and power. That's why you must either submit to the emperor's advice or suffer while attempting to be yourself.

In my own experience of fighting the empire, it has been not just a battle but an overarching war – a war of mental and emotional pain. When you speak to veterans of war, they often reflect on the difficult mental and emotional pain that has occurred rather than their visible physical injury. That's because this injury of the psyche is often too difficult to heal. The trauma is carried throughout the days and nights. This empire has at times destroyed my sleep patterns, my weight, my emotional stability, my sense of self and even my willingness to live. It's dangerous: every time I've felt I made an impact in the war, I've seen that I have been pushed back further from the side that I began.

I know it can be hard for those of you who are from a minority ethnic background or an LGBTQIA+/Queer background and experiencing bullying or challenging behaviour in your church or ministry. Some will say for the betterment of your mental health it's best for you to leave that organisation. Go somewhere that values you fully, not just aspects of you. I understand there is some privilege in this outcome, because often it can be difficult economically, relationally, and spiritually. Therefore, if this is a possible option, it's advised to investigate it gracefully.

The other option is remaining. This option can be hard without a support network of trusted people that will listen, care, and be there for you while attempting to make the organisation a safe place for all people. There are networks of like-minded people outside your workplace who can also support you. And finally, if it is safe, attempt to speak to the human resources department and to document everything. Also, make sure you are documenting every microaggression and bullying issue that has arisen at work since you started your time there. Through all of this, make sure you can pray and seek faithful advice from people with wisdom. Calm your heart and try not to be troubled. We have a God who understands and fights with and for us daily. Let's end with this prayer:

> God of the Open Doors, Open Hearts, and Open Minds,
> Establish in this Church/organisation a conscience for your people.
> Help us to treat those of different sexual orientations, gender identities, and racial groups with equity and equality.
> Forgive us when we have failed to show a radical welcome or when we have not invited others to the table.
> Change us, holy God. Imbue in us your spirit of love, honour, mercy, grace, justice, equity, and belonging.
> In the name of God, who is the creator, redeemer, and sustainer.
> Amen.

---

[1] Leyens, J. Ph., Paladino, M. P., Rodriguez, R. T., Vaes, J., Demoulin, S., Rodriguez, A. P., & Gaunt, R. (2000), 'The emotional side of prejudice: The attribution of secondary emotions to ingroups and outgroups', *Personality and Social Psychology Review*, 4, pp. 186-197.

[2] *Tackling Bullying at Work: A UNISON guide for safety reps*, https://www.unison.org.uk/content/uploads/2013/07/Online-Catalogue216953.pdf (Accessed: October 25, 2022).

17

Shunning as a Method of Control in Authoritarian Churches

STEPHEN PARSONS

There are many religious and political groups that exercise strong control over their members. Strict methods are used to enforce obedience and conformity. These may cause harm and pain, as well as being destructive of personal freedom. The top-down power that operates in such controlling groups is not always visible to the onlooker. Subtle mechanisms of coercion are in operation, and these ensure that a tight discipline is exercised over the entire group. Cults and tight political cliques have always been known to practise a range of techniques involving fear to maintain the unquestioning obedience of their members. It is alarming to discover that some church congregations are also open to using a range of covert methods of control. These allow the leadership of these churches to maintain an unchallenged dominance in managing the spiritual and material affairs of the group.

One of the ways in which the leaders of some close-knit religious or political groups keep a strict hold over their members, is by erecting high barriers between those who are 'in' and those who remain on the outside. The barriers are not, of course, necessarily physical in nature, but they act in just as effective a way. In the closed, tightly controlled Christian groups, those which resemble cults, members are conditioned not to spend much time thinking about those who are not signed up to their church or congregation. The leadership of these groups take care to provide a network of support to fulfil all the social and emotional needs of members. Their group or organisation is also presented as the only reliable place to find a safe source of teaching or moral guidance. Thus the people outside, those who may hold on to a different set of beliefs, are in some sense 'infidels' or heathen. Those on the outside of the group are not worthy of attention or concern from those who belong to the cocoon of the ideologically closed group.

The damaging way that closed Christian groups can operate is seen most clearly in the way a leadership will deal harshly with individuals who want to leave the organisation. In religious language such dissidents are referred to as apostates or backsliders. The journey that they are making out of the group will inevitably involve loosening the social bonds and attachments that may have existed for their entire lives. The shunning of such departing members is thought to be a necessary consequence of their departure, because it is only by blanking and ghosting the errant leavers that the boundaries of the community can be preserved. In leaving, these departing members represent an expression of dissatisfaction with the ideology and leadership style of the organisation. Any questioning of the leadership of this kind is clearly a threat and a challenge to their power. The ideology within a closed religious group typically only embraces a single version of truth. When questions arise about whether there might be alternative versions of truth, the leadership has to act quickly to silence the dissenting voice. The status quo in terms of the doctrine and culture of the organisation has to be preserved at all costs, and this takes precedence over dealing sympathetically with an expression of unhappiness. Disagreement with or even discussion of the group belief system cannot be entertained. The questioner or dissident must be shut down, lest their voice of complaint disturb and threaten the peace of the organisation and its management. The only remedy available to the leaders when faced with protest or discontent by a member of the group is the act of excluding or banishing them from the community. This exclusion of a dissenting voice in a religious community is deftly summed up in the word 'shunning'.

Being expelled from a Christian community is a devastating experience for the one so excluded. When the blog *Surviving Church* was set up in 2013, I was expecting to hear about individuals who had suffered through being bullied or abused in some way by leaders. The most common story of spiritual pain that I received was from those driven out of church communities because they had in some way challenged the leadership. One particular congregation where shunning and exclusion were openly practised against 'difficult' members, was the Pentecostal church of Peniel in Brentwood, Essex. The leader, Bishop Michael Reid,[1] presided over a massively wealthy congregation, but abuses of power were common. A steady stream of individuals and families left the congregation in order to escape spiritual abuse by Reid and his inner circle. Among the congregation were many families who had joined the church after living in other parts of the country. They had sold their homes and relocated to Essex in order to be close to Peniel. The children of these families were particularly tied into the ideology of the church by being forced to attend the church school on the Peniel campus. Peniel, with its community and culture, was all they had ever known. In many cases the parents of Peniel families opted to work for the church. Typically, the mother would work at the church school for no wages, while the father might be employed selling insurance through a company owned and administered by senior church members. The material rewards for working for the church were barely sufficient for their needs. Much later, these idealistic men and women discovered that, not only had they been grossly underpaid, but no provision of any kind had been made to build up a pension pot for them. Also, having lived with constant appeals for sacrificial giving to fund the ambitious building projects that the leadership under Reid was always undertaking, any capital assets members had owned had been long exhausted by these manipulating appeals to give to 'God's work'.

The experience of being shunned was destructive to these escaping or expelled from Peniel families; their well-being and happiness were impacted in at least two ways. Firstly, the individuals had been ruthlessly exploited materially, so leaving was extremely difficult on a practical level. They had been persuaded to invest so much of their time and money in the church that leaving the congregation was like giving up on an investment which they had worked hard to build up over a lifetime. It was extremely hard to begin again with new careers, and they realised that financial security would always be difficult to achieve. But it was not simply the loss of financial health that the shunned individuals and families had to endure. It was finding out that the leaders of the church had expressly forbidden their old friends to speak to them or have anything to do with them. The chief attraction of Peniel Church had been its offer of instant community and fellowship. As long as the individual or family remained in the orbit of Reid's approval, the members had always been able to rely on their acceptance by others in the church. The children also had their network of instant friends, while the parents socialised among the other parents. The strong sense of needing to belong lay at the heart of the church's appeal to these young families. They longed to be in the place that God had chosen for them and their children. To see their children lose friendships with the only children they had ever mixed with added keenly to the sense of being abandoned and shunned by their church community.

Peniel Church in Brentwood opened my eyes to the potential horrors of shunning in Christian communities. I wrote about the church on my *Surviving Church* blog, using material provided by a prominent Pentecostal lawyer, John Langlois. Langlois wrote a 200,000-word critique of the church in 2015. I also started to look at some of the academic literature on shunning. I wanted to understand better what was being said in these circles about the practice of shunning in religious settings. What I found was that within mainstream scholarship there has been a developing interest in ostracism, or what is called 'social exclusion studies'. In studying the phenomenon of rejection from a group, one strand of research involved the setting up of experimental situations where individuals were deliberately left out of a group activity. Those individuals were then asked to describe their experience of exclusion.

What seemed to me remarkable in my survey of the literature was how little the mainstream scholars in the field had been drawn to considering exclusion in a religious context. There were references to the Amish, but nothing which acknowledged the widespread use of shunning and exclusion by many religious groups, including the Jehovah's Witnesses. I am unable to say whether the situation has changed in the past ten years, but it is probably still true that ostracism in a religious setting is not well understood by professional therapists and scholars. The horrors and cruelty of the practice probably still remain largely hidden to ordinary people. My own reading and listening to the survivors of such treatment made me realise that this was indeed a very serious issue. While shunning is not abusive in the narrow definition of the word, it remains an action involving cruelty and evil of the worst kind.

The American psychology professor Kipling Williams is an acknowledged expert in the social exclusion field, and has set out four ways in which ordinary human needs are attacked by ostracism and shunning.[2] Whether or not practised in a religious context, it will have a devastating effect on its victims. It would not be an exaggeration to think of ostracism as a destructive act comparable to murder. It is sometimes described as soul-murder; not a few of its victims are driven by despair to take their own lives.

The four human needs attacked, according to Williams, by the experience of shunning are

- Belonging
- Self-esteem
- Sense of control
- Meaningful existence.

It remains for us to comment briefly on each of these four areas to indicate how seriously we should take shunning, especially when we find it being practised by religious groups. The first assault on an excluded human individual, by destroying their sense of belonging, is grievous and devastating. For some that belonging to the group may be the only experience of belonging they have ever had. Their profound need to belong is attacked and, in the words of a much-quoted essay, 'there will be pathological consequences beyond mere temporary distress'.[3]

When we consider the destruction of self-esteem that takes place in the experience of shunning, we find that the victim is often forced to doubt their own value and goodness. They are being excluded by others, and the ability to feel good about themselves is under constant attack. As an outcast, it is difficult ever to feel a strong sense of inner morale and social identity. The affirmation of the human beings around us is an important ingredient of our ability to function well mentally. If we are greeted by avoidance and silence from members of our community, it is easy to descend into absolute despair.

This silence that greets us as we attempt to engage with others also removes from us our sense of control and agency. Nothing we do or say has any effect and we are left feeling that we have no proper existence. We are, as it were, adrift in an ocean of indifference to our existence, since the wall of silence has removed from us the power to interact effectively with our surroundings.

Williams' final category, 'meaningful existence', sums up all the previous three areas of human need. Williams here discusses 'Terror Management Theory', which suggests that human beings can only deal with the fear of death by interacting with other people. With the experience of being an outcast, individuals are forced to contemplate alone the terrors and reality of dying. In a traditional society, the expulsion from the community would make physical survival hard to achieve for more than a few days.

The extremes of shunning are hopefully not found in too many places, but the potential to devastate peoples' lives by even threatening to behave in this way should be understood. This version of soul-murder can never be tolerated within a Christian framework. But while it is probably true that shunning is still relatively rare in

Christian communities, the threat of it still exists where a church leader believes that he or she knows God's will for a congregation and the individuals within it. The practice of shunning and social exclusion through the exercise of power is built into the arrogant claims of a church leader whose grasp of truth is not mingled with the Christian virtues of love, humility, and compassion.

---

[1] https://victimsofbishopmichaelreid.blogspot.com/2017/08/john-langlois-report-links.html

[2] Willams, Kipling, *Ostracism: The Power of Silence* (NY: Guilford Press, 2001).

[3] Baumeister, R. F and Leary, M. R., 'The Need to Belong: Desire for interpersonal attachments as a fundamental human motivation' in *Psychological Bulletin* 117(3), 497-529, 1995: and at https://doi.org/10.1037/0033-2909.117.3.497.

18

Cyber Bullying

CLIVE BILLENNESS

When the *New York Times* first coined the term 'Cyberbully' in an article in 1995, they could not have foreseen how toxic and widespread cyberbullying would become, not only among school students but also among adults; and how many kilometres of newsprint and gigabytes of web reports would be dedicated to it over the following quarter-century.

Cyberbullying has been defined by Susan Limber as: 'Deliberate and hostile behaviour intended to harm people using the Internet by leveraging the imbalance of power between bullies and victims.'[1] Other academics have described cyberbullying in similar terms.

This leverage of the imbalance of power may be in order to coerce or intimidate others to bend to their will, to establish and maintain their own position of authority within a group, or simply to derive satisfaction from watching others suffer.

There are some terms used in Limber's definition which are of particular note. First, that the behaviour is *deliberate* and the likely outcome is intended. Second, that it is *hostile*. The cyberbully is adopting an aggressive stance. Third, that there is an *intent* to cause *harm*. Throughout this book, the harm occasioned by being targeted by bullies has been well-documented. However, the issue of proving intent is more difficult when dealing with a case of cyberbullying where some form of sanction or disciplinary or legal proceedings is envisaged.

In the UK, however, there is legal precedent in the case of Donoghue v Stevenson ([1932] AC652) which ruled that 'You must take reasonable care to avoid acts or omissions which you can reasonably foresee would be likely to injure your neighbour'. The landmark case of Bourhill v Young ([1943] AC 92) ruled that a person must take such reasonable care as will avoid the risk of injury, and be mindful of the result of an act or omission such that injury is likely to follow such as a reasonable person would contemplate. It is therefore not necessary to prove *intent* but simply that there has been a failure to properly foresee the consequences of an act or omission.

Cyberbullying can occur in a number of different ways. The list below is not intended to be comprehensive:

1. Spreading of untrue or maliciously-inspired information or accusations about someone to third parties via email or social media. In churches, this might be extended to include printing untrue information in church bulletins or newsletters. Such acts can also be directed against members of the target's family.
2. Speculating to others about someone's behaviour or motivations based on untrue or incomplete facts. This can include unjustified criticisms about an individual's competence.
3. Bombarding someone with emails, texts, or other messages demanding actions which they cannot take or setting unrealistic timescales for a response.
4. Excluding someone from electronic lists or groups.
5. Withholding information of great importance to a person's role and then criticising them for making decisions arising from that lack of information.
6. Excluding someone from online meetings or preventing

them from expressing themselves at those meetings.

7. Publicly criticising someone without giving them any opportunity to explain or defend themselves. This might include negative comments on the organisation's website or a chat room.

These are a subset of the 'Negative Acts' in the Negative Acts Questionnaire[2] which particularly lend themselves to cyberbullying. There is one additional Negative Act which can be experienced where an organisation's email system is under the exclusive control of a third party, and individuals' private emails can be read by unauthorised persons, thereby gaining access to confidential or sensitive information.

Many attempts have been made to quantify the extent to which cyberbullying is occurring. The majority of these have focused on this form of abuse among children and adolescents, since it has always been perceived that the greatest level of internet connectedness, and therefore the capability to participate in this type of abuse, is to be found among these age groups. Since, however, anyone who was at school in 1995 would by now be in their thirties or forties, and connection to the Internet is almost universal within all age groups, this segregation by age is no longer appropriate. Indeed, it may be that the risks of cyberbullying are greater among older generations; school education programmes go to great lengths to eliminate this type of behaviour among younger internet users, whereas older people have only their own socially-acquired manners and inhibitions to discourage them.

One study of 20,000 adults conducted in New Zealand in 2019 showed that 15 per cent of respondents had been targets of cyberbullying at least once in their lifetime, and slightly more than 2 per cent reported that they had experienced it within the preceding month.[3] It is clear that while physical bullying, involving the use of some form of physical violence, is not widely experienced, many people do find themselves targeted by cyberbullies. There are reports that this form of bullying is common within church communities and may involve both individuals and large groups jointly engaging in bullying behaviour.

One of the pioneering researchers in the area of cyberbullying, Canadian teacher Bill Belsey (who, after the *New York Times,* is widely credited with introducing the term 'cyberbully' into common usage) warns that bullying must be addressed by an entire community, and highlighted as abnormal and abusive conduct.

It is widely agreed that bullies are, in the main, *made* and not *born*. The single significant exception to this are people with psychopathic traits, who, owing to their inability to empathise with others, may lack any appreciation of the severity of the consequences of their actions. It appears easier, however, to entice someone into committing or condoning acts of cyberbullying than conventional bullying.

Professors of Criminology Ronald Akers and Wesley Jennings, writing in the *Handbook of Criminological Theory,* suggest that this is due to individuals being more easily drawn into a process known as 'Social Learning'[4] by which deviant behaviour is learned from others, and that people are generally more likely to engage in deviant or criminal behaviour when they associate with other people who promote and favour behaviour of this type and offer justifications for its use. They suggest that if deviant behaviour is either condoned or goes relatively unpunished, it is more likely to be imitated. This is sometimes referred to as 'differential association' because individuals see a particular behaviour as being effective, or not being condemned. And the more someone is exposed to it, the more likely they are to adopt it. Uncontrolled, it can spread rapidly through an organisation unless treated.

Thus, one or two deviant individuals can quickly corrupt an entire organisation.

Four factors have been identified which influence the social learning of deviant behaviours:

1. **Differential Social Organisation** – the common characteristics of the group. Worship communities tend to have many things in common, not least of which is a shared expression of faith which will bring many other implied values with it.

2. **Differential Location Within An Overall Social Structure** – the perceived social position of the group within the wider community. Churches tend to be seen as having a high status within their communities. Their values can therefore be easily seen as irreproachable and easy to comply with uncritically. Organisations which have complex, or even secret, membership rituals tend to acquire an even higher level of social status. This tends to further enhance the acceptability of their values and behaviours among members.

3. **Differential Social Location within the group** – the size and organisational structure, as well as an individual's position within a group, can place pressure on that individual to conform to a deviant social norm out of fear of group rejection. If deviant behaviour is driven from a senior position within the group, this can lead to initially fearful compliance with or non-opposition to such behaviour but, since it is going unchallenged by the group's hierarchy, it can rapidly become natural behaviour.

4. **Theoretically Defined Structural Variables** – this item encompasses the many other theories about what conditions can lead to criminal or deviant behaviour, from social disorganisation, to political or theological disagreements, to internal conflict.

If these are the general factors which can cause deviant behaviour, it is necessary to consider how they can be exaggerated and aggravated in cyberspace.

It has been suggested that key factors are the opportunity for anonymity provided by electronic communications and also the potential to benefit from 'diffused responsibility', whereby individual accountability and responsibility is weakened by being part of a group activity. In simple terms, there may be too many people involved in a cyberbullying attack to punish everyone – if they can even be identified.

This is linked to the concept of 'differential reinforcement', where individuals observe and are influenced by the positive and negative consequences for others of deviant behaviour. Akers proposes that there are 4 reinforcement mechanisms to influence behaviour:

- Positive reinforcement – where the individual receives some form of reward
- Negative reinforcement – where punishments are removed
- Positive punishment – where the individual experiences some personal punishment or sanction
- Negative punishment – where the individual experiences the loss of a reward.

Where an organisation fails to deal promptly and visibly with cyberbullying, the probability increases that others will interpret this as reinforcement and feel encouraged to participate in this behaviour.

One further consideration is the extent to which individuals may be inhibited from participating in deviant acts by their own sense of right and wrong. While within a religious community one would expect the levels of self-inhibition to be very strong, these can be overcome by 'neutralisation techniques' in which an individual decides that deviant behaviour is permissible under 'certain exceptional conditions' and then convinces themselves, or is convinced by others, that such exceptional conditions now apply and therefore sets aside their normal moral standards.

So what might an organisation do to prevent or combat cyberbullying ?

The first step is for the organisation to create 'definitions' which serve to clearly show a rejection of bullying behaviours. Definitions can be Positive, Negative or Neutralising. While Positive definitions generate approval of or acceptance of bullying behaviours and Neutralising ones suggest that there are conditions under which it would be acceptable, Negative definitions exhibit clear disapproval and do not admit any circumstances under which such behaviours would be tolerated. The widespread adoption of negative definitions serves to create an environment where cyberbullying is unreservedly condemned and participation is discouraged.

It is then necessary to show publicly that indulging in cyberbullying will have negative consequences for those who engage in it. This can be achieved with a combination of positive and negative punishments. Many church denominations already have appropriate disciplinary structures, anti-bullying policies, and safeguarding procedures which can be applied where appropriate. In some cases, however, those responsible for cyberbullying may not be subject to sanction. In addition, at the time of writing this article, office-holders such as churchwardens may not be legally removed from their office in the Church of England if they are found to have been indulging in cyberbullying.

It may, however, be possible to apply 'negative

punishment' by measures like removing an individual's right to use church mailing lists, edit the website, or send out other electronic communications in the church's name. An intermediate step may be to make all their communications subject to approval by a moderator before they are accepted onto a church's systems.

In order to address 'diffuse responsibility' it must be made clear that any member of a Church found to have been participating in cyberbullying will face similar positive or negative punishment. While it may not be possible to identify the individuals concerned to the other members of the congregation, a clear message must be sent that action will be taken.

All bullying, including cyberbullying, is sinful. The Churches must therefore address their involvement in the commission of the sin if their systems, offices, or structures are being misused to perpetrate it.

---

[1]	Kowalski, R. M., Morgan C. A., Limber, S. P., 'Traditional bullying as a potential warning sign of cyberbullying', *School Psychology International* 33(5), 2012: 505-519.

[2]	Einarsen, S., Hoel, H., and Notelaers, G., 'Measuring exposure to bullying and harassment at work: Validity, factor structure and psychometric properties of the Negative Acts Questionnaire Revised.' *Work & Stress*, [e-journal] 23(1) 2009, pp.24-44.

[3]	Privitera, C. and Campbell, M.A., 'Cyberbullying: the new face of workplace bullying?', CyberPsychol Behav Aug;12(4) 2009 :395-400. https://pubmed.ncbi.nlm.nih.gov/19594381/

[4]	Piquero, Alex R. (ed.) *The Handbook of Criminological Theory* (Hoboken, NJ: John Wiley & Sons, 2016).

19

Bullying in Religious Settings: The Impact on Faith

JONATHAN
ABERNETHY-BARKLEY

Aged two, I was welcomed to the faith through a sprinkling of water and the vows of parents.

Aged eight, I took those vows and promises and made them my own.

Aged eleven, surrounded by family, that faith saw public profession and admission to church membership.

Aged eighteen, I began to doubt.

Aged twenty-one, I found my way back.

Aged twenty-three, I began to train for ministry.

Aged twenty-three … I experienced bullying by the people I had placed my trust in, and found on the fringes of society the embrace I had expected from the seminary. Instead of being ministered to by ministers with clerical collars, my minister walked in high heeled shoes, had a quick wit that could light up rooms, had a face full of makeup and a wardrobe to die for!: the drag queen, Lady Portia Di'Monte (the best face never to be discovered). It was she who showed me grace and acceptance. It was at her weekly service, a karaoke night called 'Sunday Service', that she preached a gospel of inclusion and welcome.

I give you this background, not as chronology, though of course it is that too, but to show that the premise of this book is not alien or remote for me, but is my lived reality too. I know how it feels when your faith world crumbles into rubble, I know how disillusioned it can make you feel, I too have cried those rivers of tears, I too have questioned my faith. I have seen at times my faith abandoned, continued, or emerging in a new and different form, which meant that I could live and breathe beyond the confines of sacred buildings, beyond the Sunday sermon. My faith, it lives for me in the quiet waters beside shorelines, it smells like the dew on fresh grass, it resonates in the lyrics of popular music, and it tastes like the best glass of red wine in the world.

Before elaborating further on the impact that bullying in Christian cultures can have on a person's faith journey, I must address the elephant in the room. I have alluded to being bullied myself while at seminary, but haven't said why. The answer is simple and straightforward, and it is as old as time: difference. For two millennia now, those who don't quite fit the mould of what those in positions of power deem to be the 'right kind' of Christian faith are asked to leave, or treated in a way that makes them feel so uncomfortable that they decide to leave. They may be a woman, a person of colour, or a member of the LGBTQI+ community. My chief sin was seeking to live an authentic faith, to be the person that my creator made me to be. My queerness, which was as much part of my life as my faith was, seemed to be a threat, a challenge.

I should add that it wasn't that anyone actually had the audacity to ask me if I was gay, at least, not at the start; but the very whiff of my perceived sexuality was enough to set the hares running. The hunt for any supporting 'evidence' that could render a guilty verdict went into overdrive. The bullying took many forms, such as Facebook stalking, or offering opinions that weren't asked for such as, 'maybe someone like you would be better suited to the art college rather than a theological college'. The pressure, the hurt, the pain, and the bullying intensified, physically and emotionally – I became gradually anorexic, I drank to numb the hurt, but the relief never lasted long, and I only drank more. My experience of bullying within a Christian setting or culture led me to some very dark places.

While my experience is unique to me, I dare say that it is not unfamiliar to many. As Gansevoort and Sremac observe:

> In the care of trauma, human existence is characterized by brokenness, struggle, and fragmentariness, which asks for a process of making sense of one's traumatic experience in the light of one's own bibliography, identity and religious beliefs or worldview. Dealing with these ultimate questions and existential experiences is a process with a highly individual character, which forms part of lived religion.[1]

It is that motif of commonality of shared experience and pain, to which I now turn in more detail.

Faith Abandoned

Women Talking, a 2018 novel by Miriam Toews, fictionalises events occurring between 2005 and 2009 in a remote Mennonite colony, where more than one hundred women and girls were raped by what many believed to be ghosts or demons. The women's accounts are dismissed as wild female imagination. The novel details the imagined response of the women when they discover the truth: that they were being systematically abused by their husbands, sons, and relatives. The women discuss whether they should remain in the colony or leave, drawing up a list of pros and cons for each option. Ona Friesen, one of the characters, remarks during this process, *'when we have liberated ourselves, we will have to ask ourselves who we are'*.

Women Talking identifies that it is from a position of adult experience and understanding that the women in the novel begin to grapple with what has occurred to them, and is happening around them in the lives of others.

For the individual who has been bullied, a myriad of emotions, feelings, and conflicting ideas may flood the psyche. To have what was once certain shaken by the behaviour of another can lead the recipient into a landscape of greyness, where there once was light and colour. The response might be to walk away, to abandon, to leave; though one must remember that in doing so the journey might only be beginning. The heavy lifting and hard yards of asking yourself who you are now that you have left may lead to more dark nights of the soul and struggle.

Faith continued

Elisabeth Elliot comments, 'sometimes life is so hard and you can only do the next thing. God will meet you there'. Sometimes the next thing means staying where you are, and continuing with the faith that in the hands of the perpetrator, has been turned against you.

There is a wonderful thing about ritual and liturgy; it requires as much or as little on your part as you wish to contribute or bring to the table. For some the comfort comes from knowing that the words printed on the page in front of you, or in the *Book of Common Order,* have been a source of comfort, reassurance, and joy for the countless generations that have come before. Throughout the ages the words have been uttered and the Spirit has moved, just like, in the Genesis account, it hovered over the deep and a world was born.

For some who have experienced bullying and abuse firsthand, remaining, sometimes not having the words, conviction of heart or 'faith', is okay. Even if they don't have the words, if the syllables are not easily formed on the tongue and given voice, others around them can say them aloud. The abused or bullied can hear those worshipping in the same place, encounter something of the mystery of faith as they listen, and be nourished and fed – even if it feels like mere morsels dropped from a table, rather than the banquet that was once known.

For others, there will be a sense of 'the church is not God, and thank God for that', meaning that the faith they have is not tied up in a person or a building, but is a gift that moves freely between creator and created. In spite of what they have encountered, they can still connect with the divine, and see their faith strengthened, grow and be renewed to be something that continues to flourish, even in desert places.

Faith Emerging

For some, the choice between leaving or remaining is nuanced. The search for life and faith, post-abuse, can lead to a third way (as a famous politician once said). They see their faith emerge in a different form, or in different things. C. R. Benyei observes,

> in their stories of healing survivors have reported religious confusion as they have struggled to make a positive life after years of abuse, they have searched for a God of love and power, but their search is difficult because so many images of God are negative.[2]

As the result of the bullying the God of stained-glass windows no longer seems approachable, relatable, lovable; but being human and being wired for connection, the dedication, the loyalty, the persevering of faith is manifested in different things and or places. Walks on a beach become sacred, the time spent reading poetry or novels replaces Bible study and church services and provides equal food for thought. The mowing of the local cricket lawn has a rhythm and a beauty and a song, that once was piped from an organ or sung by a choir. New ways of understanding and encountering the world and what it means to be human, from nature to the sublime to the banal, all provide that sense of grounding and comfort that faith once did.

By way of conclusion: just as every person's faith experience and journey is unique, how an individual responds to bullying experienced within a faith community/culture is equally unique. That being said, this chapter has explored three common responses: those for whom as a result of the experience faith is abandoned; those for whom faith is continued; and those who see their faith emerging in a new form. This chapter began with me reflecting on my personal lived experience of being bullied within a Christian setting. I am happy to confirm that for me, while in the moment the bullying was experienced I had a crisis of faith, my faith continues, burning brightly and beautifully just like the rainbow after a storm, in spite of the experiences I encountered.

---

[1]   Ganzevoort, R. Ruard and Srdjan, Sremac (eds.), *Trauma and Lived Religion: Transcending the Ordinary* (Palgrave Studies in Lived Religion and Societal Challenges) (New York: Springer International Publishing AG, 2019).

[2]   Benyei, C. R., *Understanding clergy misconduct in religious systems: Scapegoating, family secrets, and the abuse of power* (New York: Routledge, 1998).

20

Watching Blood Flow Under the Door

ALISON KENNEDY

On Easter Monday 1916, a group of Irish republicans launched an armed insurrection in Dublin. The initial reaction from the local population was ambivalent. But when the British government responded by executing the rebels, the response was one of shocked disbelief. One Irish woman commented: 'It was like watching a stream of blood come from under a closed door.'[1]

This powerful image was offered by someone whose clergy partner had been a target of workplace bullying so severe that the cleric concerned felt pressured into resigning and signing a non-disclosure agreement. For the partner, it encapsulated the same feeling of powerlessness that the Irish woman hearing of the executions behind closed doors experienced: 'I have no power and no voice.'

This chapter documents the experience of those whose clergy partners have been targets of bullying. Collated from a series of fifteen interviews and written submissions from the spouses of eleven male and four female clergy (whose identities have been obscured to protect anonymity), it makes no claim to be exhaustive. It acknowledges the limitations of being a small-scale qualitative study and raises as many questions as it answers. Its modest aim is simply to give a voice to those clergy partners who have suffered as what Rory Remer terms 'secondary victims'[2] of bullying, whose experience has been under-researched.

The bullying described was meted out by laity, colleagues, and senior clergy towards clergy at varying levels of seniority. Their partners were – and still are, in several cases – impacted physically, mentally, emotionally, and spiritually by witnessing the effects of bullying on their partners:

> 'It has impacted my sleep. I have needed to access mental health treatment.'

> 'The physical symptoms are huge. We thought we had COVID, we were so tired.'

> 'None of it ever leaves you. We thought the house was bugged. I feel frightened to pick up the phone.'

There is something particular about being a secondary victim; the one witnessing the 'blood run under the door'. Partners described the sense of helplessness without any sort of resolution:

> 'My husband was able to talk about it with some of the leadership. There was a sense of prolonged resolution. But I haven't had that cathartic experience of being able to do that. It's really challenging and very emotionally difficult.'

> 'I couldn't protect my family from this and that has had long-term consequences for our health and our children.'

Very commonly, partners described their shock about experiencing bullying within a church community:

'The challenge for me is this dichotomy of being in a community that are supposed to love you, but actually it's the opposite.'

'You can't rely on them being good people just because they're Christians. It is a wicked shock.'

But the shock was not limited to those within the church community. In one case, where the severe situation required legal intervention, the lawyer questioned:

'Why is the diocese not supporting its own?'

Several related the effect that it had on their family:

'It impacts on the family because he gets angry and he gets angry with me ... We're both more cynical, tired and grumpy.'

'I feel I have sacrificed my family on the altar of the church.'

'One of our children wanted to hire an assassin.'

What was perhaps surprising was that, while commonly partners were angry with the church, very rarely did a partner blame God for what had happened. The faith of the children in the family, however, was sometimes impacted:

'We got through it. But the children were all stressed because of what was happening ... The kids are very resilient and very close-knit [but it also] put off my daughter going into the priesthood.'

'I live with a deep grief that my eldest cannot even believe in God.'

In other cases, partners themselves became the target of bullying, as a way of continuing the bullying of the cleric:

'There was a smear campaign which went back into my personal history ... I was physically intimidated by a large man ... I became really ill ...'

Having given a detailed account of 'mobbing' (where a small group work together to intimidate, harass, and demoralise the target) the partner described feeling driven to the point of suicide:

'The stress levels were so great, I stood on the balcony and ... I felt totally and utterly abandoned by God and the church.'

One partner described being physically attacked by a member of the congregation:

'I was told that I had to stop going to church. I stopped going, particularly after I was hit. [The bully] walked into the vicarage kitchen and hit me. It was so weird; I wasn't sure it had really happened ... This caused thirty years of agoraphobia and panic attacks. I think I'm paying for it now. My health has deteriorated.'

One particular issue facing clergy families is that frequently their home is tied to their work. Being given a house which is often larger than those of parishioners and for which maintenance is provided is often seen as a perk of the role – and was acknowledged as such by many partners (although some also reported how difficult it was to get the property maintained). However, this dynamic of 'living over the shop' created additional pressures. Leaving a post is a very costly and difficult exercise, involving not only the loss of livelihood but much more besides:

> 'If the post fails, you look for a new life. It's my social life, my friends, my voluntary work, my home. It's everything, isn't it?'

One respondent compared it to the situation of being an armed forces wife:

> 'You're stuck. We have no property so we can't go anywhere. If we could have left, we would. But we don't have any choice.'

In addition, when bullying was experienced, partners felt that their homes were 'contaminated' by the bullying, from which they felt there was no escape:

> 'On the whole, I enjoy it, but when it goes wrong, there's no escape. You're surrounded by it.'

> 'I did really fear for my safety in my own home.'

> 'It's quite hard to keep work and home separate. In the end, we only talked about it in the study.'

This highlights the fact that boundaries between home and work for clergy are not as clearly defined as they are in most other professions, which can create a dynamic in which partners and families feel that a power is held over them that can be abused:

'People think we're their private property.'

'Someone else has the keys to your house.'

'There's this constant feeling of being watched.'

'The house has to be in a state where people can always come in.'

While most reported working hard at maintaining good professional boundaries between home and work, others reported that parishioners did not always respect those boundaries:

'I was pinned against a wall by a member of the congregation and asked: "Can't you get him to change the buttons on his cassock?".'

Several partners also reported how witnessing a partner being bullied severely impacted their marital relationships:

'I feel the church has almost destroyed us.'

'It led to tension between us. He used to be quite laid back – he used to have such a *joie de vivre* about him – but it just rubbed off. He lost his joy … It was physically damaging. He was so afraid. It was so horrible to see … He was really, really wounded … He's not the same person. He's much more cynical and he's exhausted and really, really grumpy … I nearly left him…'

Several partners talked about the complex question of vocation. This sense of vocation is not limited to the clergy person. Clergy partners often have their own sense of vocation to their role, either as the member of a clergy couple, or in their own right as individuals (several clergy partners reported giving high levels of practical support to their partner's ministry, in which they found fulfilment and satisfaction). In addition, given that most clergy roles are linked to the family home, the sense of commitment (sometimes expressed in terms of vocation) from a partner is often integral to – and therefore inseparable from – the ministry. It is therefore easy to understand why a partner would feel directly affected by the bullying of their partner:

> 'Stuff that was an attack on him felt like an attack on me.'

> 'It makes me question why we bothered to come here; it makes you question your own sense of vocation and calling.'

Understandably, moving to a new post brings particular anxieties for those whose clergy partners have been targets of bullying:

> 'You carry things with you … Am I doing something wrong? How do I know it won't happen again? How do I stop it happening again? How do I deal with my feelings of anger so that they don't spill over into the new place?'

> 'You always live with the knowledge and fear that it could all start again and that this aberration may just be an illusion of peace.'

Partners craved quality peer support, recognising that such support had become more complex to provide.

Historically, Anglican clergy wives were often supported by the bishop's wife. That model is still operating in some dioceses, but this one-size-fits-all model no longer serves a model of ministry in which women are ordained and often both partners are working (never mind the elephant-in-the-room situation in which a partner is of the same sex as the cleric …).

Where peer support *is* still provided by the bishop's wife, there are inevitable conflicts of interest:

> 'In this diocese, I'm not aware of any support for clergy spouses. In our previous diocese, the bishop's wife organised events and sent welcome cards. But you couldn't say anything negative or challenge something. You couldn't say anything that reflected negatively on your partner in those gatherings, especially when posts were being cut. The culture was suppressing.'

> 'I would never take a problem to the hierarchy. The response even from the wives of senior clergy is: we coped, you can cope.'

Several partners reported feeling let down by the lack of pastoral care from the church:

> 'When things were really bad, no one asked what was happening to us. We were threatened with being evicted. The bishop concerned basically tried it on. He tested out whether I knew my rights about freehold.'

The partners' experience of powerlessness at witnessing bullying in church was heightened when situations in which bullying was known about were not tackled by church authorities:

'And the awful thing is that [the bully] is still there. How is the next person supposed to cope?'

'The diocese has been very supportive but all they have is kind words. They've told us: "You can't take a case out against a lay person".'

In more than one instance, the issue had a long history which had not been resolved:

'[My spouse] couldn't battle fifty to sixty years of control power.'

'If we'd had the support of our diocese, it would have been very different. I think the diocese were frightened to challenge the rich and the church structures ... People wrote letters on our behalf, but never got a reply ...'

'What I wanted from the hierarchy was that they would take a mirror and hold it up to the bully. Sometimes good pastoral care is confronting someone with the truth of their behaviour and the consequences for other people.'

The brutal suppression of the Easter Rising in Dublin marked a turning point. It galvanised support for Irish independence. For those witnessing the bullying of their clergy partners, it also marked a turning point:

'The disproportionate violence of the Easter Rising caused the Irish people to lose confidence in the British government. I feel that I have also lost confidence in the leadership of the church through this.'

Others report:

> 'It has made me very cynical about the church; it's a very graceless organisation.'

> 'I have no respect for the Church of England. I have no respect of the hierarchy. I still have a faith, but I don't care if I never go to another church.'

The Church of England reached a turning point in the form of the IICSA (Independent Inquiry into Child Sexual Abuse) report. Responding to the report, the Church gave the following assurance about safeguarding:

> 'We acknowledge our poor response to victims and survivors. We must ensure that our response to victims and survivors is meaningful, compassionate and personal'.[3]

Bullying in the church is an own goal. As the stories of clergy partners testify, it harms not only the clergy but their partners, their families and church as a whole. A 'meaningful, compassionate and personal' response to bullying, also, is badly needed.

---

[1]   Anonymous Irish woman, quoted in Kee, Robert, *Ireland: A Television History*, Episode 8: 'Rising,' screened 20 January 1981, BBC/RTE).

[2]   Bremer, R, in Catherall, D.R., *Handbook of Stress, Trauma, and the Family* (Abingdon: Routledge, 2004).

[3]   Gibbs, J., *Response to the publication of the final report of the Independent Inquiry into Child Sexual Abuse (IICSA)*. 2022. https://www.churchofengland.org/media/press-releases/response-publication-final-report-independent-inquiry-child-sexual-abuse-iicsa

21

Bullying and Harassment in the Church of England: Legal Remedies

RICHARD SCORER AND CECILIA DAVIES

Note: Although this chapter focuses on the law and the established Church of England, readers will find much of it more widely applicable. (The editors)

Over the past two decades increasing evidence has emerged of abuse, bullying, and harassment in Anglican churches in the UK. In a powerful piece in the *Church Times* in February 2024, Revd Janet Fife described her experience of sexual abuse and harassment by a senior male cleric at Bradford Cathedral, and the repeated obstacles she encountered in getting accountability from church authorities. As the book *Letters to a Broken Church* confirms, her experiences are far from uncommon. There have also been cases where individuals have been wrongly accused and have experienced similar institutional denial and cover-up. In 2021 the Church of England was criticised after a priest, Fr Alan Griffin, took his own life following a mishandled inquiry into child abuse allegations. When Griffin died in 2020 he had spent a year under investigation without ever having seen the allegations against him. The coroner at his inquest noted that the claims were 'supported by no complainant, no witness and no accuser'. These cases suggest that significant institutional obstacles can be encountered within the Church of England and its sister Anglican churches in the UK both by those who suffer abuse and harassment and those who might have been wrongly accused. The purpose of this chapter is to examine the civil legal remedies available in secular courts for those affected, and to identify areas for reform. As this chapter examines civil legal remedies, those interested in canon law and Clergy Conduct Measure aspects will need to consult other sources. This is intended as a brief overview only; the law is complex, particularly where clergy are concerned, and anyone experiencing assault, bullying, or harassment in their workplace, or believing themselves to have been wrongly accused of it, should seek specialist legal advice. This article is not a substitute for such advice, and should not be relied upon as formal advice – it is intended to be an outline exploration of the law and a pointer to reforms that should be considered.

Employment status of clergy

Before considering civil remedies it is important to highlight an important issue in this context; the employment status of clergy. Many of those affected by abuse, bullying, and harassment in the Church are either clergy themselves, or have been abused, bullied, or harassed by clergy. Of course, not everyone who works in the Church is a member of the clergy. Many of those who are not – for example a secretary employed by a diocese – will have a contract of employment. Some clergy, for example those working as chaplains in secular organisations, may also work under a contract of employment. However, the majority of clergy in the Church of England hold their ecclesiastical office under Common Tenure as created by the Ecclesiastical Offices Terms of Service Legislation Measure (2009). Clergy under Common Tenure are office holders and not under a contract of employment. One consequence is that their rights, particularly in an employment law context, are more limited. For example, they have a right of appeal to an Employment Tribunal if removed from office on grounds of capability, but no right to claim constructive dismissal. While under Common Tenure it is possible for clergy to make use of a grievance procedure, there is no resort to an Employment Tribunal if an office holder is dissatisfied at the end of the grievance procedure. A detailed examination of the special position of clergy is outside the scope of this article, and many issues have to be considered on a case-by-case and fact-sensitive basis. However, the fact that clergy are not employees can have legal consequences both in respect of their rights to claim when affected by events at work, and in respect of the liability of the Church itself.

Bullying and harassment – civil remedies

As noted above, there is increasing evidence that bullying and harassment in the Church is a widespread problem. In terms of legal remedies, there is no tort of bullying as such, whether at common law or under statute. (A 'tort' is a civil wrong which gives rise to a cause of action in law.) Therefore 'bullying' is not a cause of action on its own. Bullying is also not defined under UK law. However, the Advisory, Conciliation, and Arbitration Service (ACAS) describes bullying as behaviour from one or more individuals to another that is: malicious, insulting, intimidating, abusive, an abuse or misuse of power or process that undermines, humiliates or causes physical or emotional harm to another.

Bullying therefore can involve a single incident or a regular pattern of unwanted behaviour, and can take place via emails, letters, phone calls, face-to-face, or on social media platforms.

Unlike bullying, however, harassment is defined under UK law. Section 26 (1) of the Equality Act 2010 (EQA10) defines harassment as: unwanted conduct related to a protected characteristic that has the purpose or effect of violating a person's dignity or creating an intimidating, degrading, humiliating or offensive environment.

Although recognition has also been given in many workplace environments to bullying and harassment that is not attributed to a protected characteristic, what is unlawful under EQA10 is harassment that is related to a protected characteristic. EQA10 defines protected characteristics as 'age, disability, gender reassignment, marriage and civil partnership, race, religion or belief, sex and sexual orientation'. Pregnancy and maternity are not included within this list; however the Equality and Human Rights Commission (EHRC) published technical guidance in January 2020 on sexual harassment and harassment at work which provides that 'harassing somebody because of pregnancy would be harassment related to sex'.

Harassment can take many forms. The EHRC guidance provides a definition of 'unwanted conduct' and covers a wide range of behaviours, for example: spoken words, banter, written words, social media posts, imagery, graffiti, physical gestures, jokes and pranks, mimicry, acts of affecting a person's surroundings, aggressive and physical behaviour towards a person or their property.

Furthermore, the EHRC recognises that harassment can be psychological, physical, and/or sexual; be a single instance or more systematic patterns of behaviour; be amongst colleagues, superiors, and subordinates or by third parties; and range from minor to serious acts that can include criminal offences that require the intervention of public authorities. Section 26 (4) EQA10 provides that in determining whether conduct has the purpose and effect to constitute harassment the victim's own perception has to be taken into account. The conduct must be a violation of their dignity, or behaviour which creates an intimidating, hostile, degrading, humiliating, or offensive environment for the victim. Sexual harassment is specifically defined under section 26(2) EQA10 and occurs when a person harasses another individual if they engage in: unwanted conduct of a sexual nature and the conduct has the purpose of violating that person's dignity or creating an intimidating, hostile, degrading, humiliating or offensive environment.

The EHRC EQA10 code of practice provides that the unwanted conduct of a sexual nature can cover: verbal, non-verbal, or physical conduct including unwelcome sexual advances, touching, forms of sexual assault, sexual jokes, displaying pornographic photographs or drawings, or sending emails with material of a sexual nature.

Turning to the issue of vicarious liability, Section 109 (1) EQA10 defines the liability of employers and principals. It provides that 'anything done by a person in the course of their employment must also be treated as done by the employer'. It is irrelevant that an employer or principal did not know of or did not approve of the act done. If a discriminatory act of harassment has taken place during the course of a person's employment, the employer is legally responsible for the actions of the person who carried out the discriminatory act. If this is disputed by an employer, the employer must show that it took reasonable steps to prevent the conduct or from doing anything from that description.

Also relevant in this area is the Protection from

Harassment Act (PHA) 1997. Under section 1 PHA 1997 a person must not pursue a course of conduct which amounts to harassment of another or which they know would amount to harassment. Section 7(3) PHA 1997 defines the 'course of conduct' under the Act: it must involve conduct on at least two occasions in relation to a single person or conduct in relation to two or more persons on at least one occasion in relation to each of those persons. Section 4 PHA 1997 provides protection for an employee where a person whose course of conduct causes another to fear, on at least two occasions, that violence will be used against him is guilty of an offence if he knows or ought to know that his course of conduct will cause another so to fear on each of those occasions. For the purposes of the Act the conduct needs to have been particularly egregious and close to the type of conduct that can lead to criminal charges. Breach of sections 1 and 7 may give rise to a claim in civil proceedings by the person who is or may be the victim of the course of conduct in question. Breach of section 4 is a criminal offence liable to imprisonment and/or a fine.

The advantage of bringing a claim under PHA 1997 is that an employee does not have to prove that harassment was due to a protected characteristic. In addition the employee may be able to obtain a restraining injunction which is not available under the EQA10 and within the ET. However, civil claims under PHA 1997 are subject to an unextendable 6-year limitation period, so any claim will be extinguished if not issued within that time period.

The availability of some of the remedies just referenced can also be affected by the employment status of clergy. There is nothing to stop clergy in the Church of England who suffer assault and harassment from deploying either the common law tort of assault (trespass to the person) or using the Protection from Harassment

Act 1997, although the use of both is subject to time limits as discussed above. The use of other statutory remedies, particularly involving EQA, is a much more complex issue. The case of Reverend D Green v Lichfield Diocesan Board of Finance ([2023] UKET 2409635/2022), where the primary issue was the extent to which a stipendiary curate had standing to bring complaints before an employment tribunal of detrimental treatment because of making protected disclosures (whistleblowing) and disability discrimination (based on a perception that he was disabled by reason of autism), illustrates some of the complexities. Again, therefore, the employment status of clergy has the potential to impact on the remedies available.

Wrongful allegations – civil remedies

The issue of wrongful allegations has recently attracted increased attention. 'Wrongful allegations' is used in this context as a catch-all term to embrace all allegations of abuse which are factually incorrect, ranging from allegations which are malicious/deliberately false, to allegations which are simply mistaken, to allegations which are partly true but exaggerated. Given the methodological problems in defining what qualifies as a wrongful allegation, there are widely diverging views regarding prevalence. However, it is recognised that wrongful allegations of abuse can cause harm to those unfairly accused. Depending on the circumstances, there are a range of potential legal remedies, for example:

- an action for libel/defamation;
  where criminal proceedings have been brought based on wrongful allegations, an action for malicious prosecution; or
- where an employer mismanages an investigation into

wrongful allegations, a personal injury claim against the employer based on negligence and/or breach of the implied contractual term of trust and confidence between employer and employee.

Where the focus is on the Church's treatment of the wrongly accused individual, the last type of remedy may be particularly relevant. An example of organisational accountability for mismanagement of an investigation into allegations of abuse is Gogay v Hertfordshire CC ([2000] I.R.L.R. 703 CA (Civ Div)). In this case the Court of Appeal upheld a judge's decision that a local authority was in breach of the implied contractual duty of trust and confidence in suspending a residential care worker pending an investigation into allegations of child abuse. It did not follow that an employee should not be suspended, because the local authority has reasonable grounds for making enquiries into allegations of child abuse. But the court held that a distinction should be drawn between the process of investigating whether a child is at risk of significant harm, and the process of dealing with an employee who is alleged to be implicated in that risk. Hale LJ acknowledged the fact that where there is a conflict between the interests of a child in a council's care and the interests of an employee, 'the interests of the child should prevail. But the employee is entitled to something better than the "knee-jerk" reaction which occurred in this case.' The Court of Appeal upheld an award of damages to the care worker in respect of psychiatric illness brought on by the employer's breach of contract in suspending her.

It is not difficult to think of analogous situations in a church context: the tragic case of Father Griffin would appear to have been more egregious. But again, a member of the clergy seeking such a remedy may encounter the difficulty identified above, namely the lack of any employment contract with the Church. Because of Common Tenure the clergy member, who is an office holder, has to use the complaint measures built into that legislative framework, rather than relying on express or implied contractual terms as an employee would be able to do.

Conclusion

Anglican Churches in England and Wales have a systemic problem of abuse, bullying, and harassment, and also sometimes a problem of wrongful allegations. In this context it is particularly important that all those affected have clear and simple routes to civil redress, but this is not always the case. One of the issues which acts as an obstacle to redress – although not the only one – is the peculiar legal status of clergy. Issues of this kind which add to the cost and complexity of legal action can act as a deterrent to those seeking accountability. A healthier culture based on accountability for wrongdoing would seek to remove these obstacles rather than entrench them.

22

What Are the Churches Doing About Bullying?

ANNE LEE

If you think you are a target of bullying there are three important things you need to do:

1. Make sure you have a group of supportive friends around you – friends you can talk to about what is happening to you.
2. Make notes. It is really important that you have contemporaneous notes of what happened, who said what, where and when, and who was there.
3. Do not confront the perpetrator. It will almost certainly make things worse.

A variety of people and institutions have tried to help with the resolution of bullying and harassment within faith groups. In 1994 the MSF Union (Manufacturing, Science and Finance) set up a Faith Workers branch to offer support to any faith worker who needed it, for whatever reason. It was MSF which published the results of the first survey into the bullying of women priests in 1998. Following a number of mergers, the Faith Workers branch is now a part of the union Unite.[1] It is open, not only to clergy, but to all employees and office holders of any faith organisation. In 2010 Unite put out a press release saying that 'clergy bullying (is) rife'.[2] The Faith Workers branch has a helpline which offers support to their members, and they also have a very helpful booklet on their website: *What if the worst happens? A Guide for members*, with the helpline phone number displayed prominently on the front cover. Five pages of this booklet relate to bullying and harassment, what targets should do and where they should go for help, and with further information given on another seven pages.

Church of England

The first survey which noted that bullying was happening to newly ordained women priests was published in 1998; a second, larger, survey published in 2000 corroborated this evidence. Since then there has been very little attempt to gauge the importance of dealing with bullying in the Church other than a few masters' or doctoral theses. It is reported that one bishop, on being asked if a researcher could conduct some research in his diocese, replied, 'No, because you might pick up problems, which I would then have to deal with.' It was encouraging that he thought such a survey might pick up on problems, and also that if it did he would need to act. However, it is disappointing that he therefore did not want any research done.

Between 2003 and 2007 there were a number of articles in the national and international press about bullying within the church which resulted in questions about bullying being asked in General Synod.

The Church of England is 'by law established'. One consequence of this is that changes in the laws of the Church of England have to be approved by the UK Parliament. Another consequence is that a member of parliament (MP) of the party then in government is appointed the Second Church Estates Commissioner and has to answer in parliament questions about the affairs of the Church of England from any MP. This position exists to maintain the statutory accountability of the Church; it seeks to provide a link between government and Parliament on the one hand and the established Church on the other.

Bullying in the Church of England has therefore been the subject of questions in Parliament. For example, on 13th May 2003 Ben Chapman MP asked Sir Stuart Bell MP, then Second Estate Church Commissioner, to make a statement on the measures taken to combat bullying in the Church. Sir Stuart responded that

> a number of Church of England dioceses have produced their own guidelines for clergy on bullying and harassment and the Convocations of Canterbury and York will publish guidelines on professional conduct later this year.

Sadly, no dioceses produced their own guidelines in 2003 and the promised guidelines on professional conduct did not mention bullying. From whom had Sir Stuart Bell received this false information? When challenged, he did not reply.

The Deployment, Remuneration, and Conditions of Service Committee of the Archbishops' Council (DRACS) produced *Dignity at Work* in 2008, specifically to address the issue of bullying in the Church with sample policies and procedures. Copies were sent to all bishops, archdeacons, diocesan clergy, lay chairs, and diocesan secretaries, with a request that copies were sent to all area or rural deans. Unfortunately this did not happen in any diocese. Following a phone call to check if it had been done, one diocesan secretary said, 'Oh, we've got lots of copies here. We did not know what to do with them.' The letter was perfectly clear. The *Dignity at Work* (2008)

Report became out of date with the introduction of the Equalities Act in 2010. There was no attempt to revise it until 2017. No revised version has been produced.

A page on the Church of England website states: 'Every diocese should have its own dignity at work policy and anti-bullying and harassment policy'.[3] The web page has two sample policies, from the Dioceses of Norwich (2016) and Derby (2018).

The Dignity at Work Policy from the Diocese of Norwich has the strapline: 'A diocesan commitment to encourage and sustain healthy and enriching relationships.' This is a clear indication that their policy is embedded in relationship. This policy is excellent. However, the policy from the Diocese of Derby continues to suggest that the target should initially try to 'sort out matters informally' (p. 7) with or without support from another person. Although research has shown that mediation is not appropriate for the resolution of bullying, four and a half pages of the Derby policy (Appendix A) relate to mediation. In one chapter of this book a respondent was reported as saying 'Being asked to be in the same room as my perpetrator is like being asked to be in the same room as my rapist'.

A faith workers' wellbeing survey (completed on 31 October 2025) of members of CEECA (Church of England Employee and Clergy Advocates) showed that 59 per cent of those responding were clergy office holders. Of the respondents that had retired, 57 per cent had retired earlier than their state pension age, 24 per cent giving their reason for retiring early as bullying and harassment. In addition, 35 per cent of the respondents said they are considering leaving their job in the next 12 to 24 months: 17 per cent gave the reason as bullying and harassment. Moreover 37 per cent (248) of all respondents said that they had experienced bullying and harassment in the last

12 months, 29 per cent had suffered verbal abuse, and 23 per cent had suffered discrimination (harassment) based on a protected characteristic. The remaining 11 per cent had been threatened with, or actually received, physical violence. 90 per cent of the respondents (551) reported suffering from stress at work; the major cause for 59 per cent was due to lack of support, while 31% said the major cause was being bullied and/or harassed.

It is clear that the Church of England is trying to put dealing with bullying on their agenda, but there has been insufficient engagement with the research and with experts in this field, and probably with other Churches, to know what help is actually needed and what works. Yet again collaboration across all fields seems as though it could be the best way forward.

Methodist Church

The Methodist Church has taken a different route and is looking at dealing with bullying and harassment positively, concentrating on the wellbeing of their ministers, staff and members. (The Church of England wellbeing policy is only about clergy.) A wellbeing advisor was appointed in 2008 and in 2017 a report was produced, *Positive Working Together*. At the same time as the report was released a series of webinars were given which are now on the Methodist Church website for anyone to participate in:

https://www.methodist.org.uk/safeguarding/webinars/bullying-webinars/

- Webinar 1: Tackling Bullying, Changing Culture, Enabling Positive Relationships
- Webinar 2: Reconciling Communities: Living Well with Difference
- Webinar 3: Addressing Bullying through Justice, Dignity and Solidarity.

A series of pages on their website[4] explain, 'here you will find information and resources on health and wellbeing issues and useful links to sources of advice.' Another series of web pages explores positive working together. Called 'The Methodist Way of Peace' it starts:

> Within the church we believe that everyone should be enabled to flourish to become the people God created them to be. Promoting positive working relationships is a key part of enabling individuals and communities to flourish.
>
> Also on the website are links to two one-day programmes: Growing Through Change and Conflict; and Responding to Bullying and Harassment Behaviour. The strapline is, 'this programme promotes good working relationships and ways to manage bullying and harassing behaviour within the life of our churches and faith communities.'

Baptist Church

The Baptist Union of Great Britain (BUGB) has a guide (2024): '*Preventing bullying and harassment. A Guide for ministers and church leaders*'.[5] It is subtitled, 'Helping Ministers and church leaders to understand what constitutes bullying and harassment.' Not all Baptist churches will use this guide as Baptist churches are independent. Members of the BUGB cannot be required to use this guide.

One important feature of the guide is that it mentions patterns of behaviour. This is a very important point. If there are allegations of bullying or harassment, the first thing which should be done is consider whether there are any patterns of behaviour: Has this congregation had a problem before? Have the target or the perpetrator ever had a problem before? Answers to these questions might demonstrate an issue with the culture of the church, a culture which church members have taken upon themselves.

United Reformed Church

The United Reformed Church (URC) has an online guide(6), 'Appendix X, Good Practice 5' dated 2020[6].

The guide starts:

1. The United Reformed Church acknowledges that bullying and harassment do occur within local churches and the wider councils. It is important that people should know where to find help if they believe themselves to have been bullied, and that those responsible for pastoral care should be vigilant for signs that bullying may be occurring. These guidelines are offered to enable the parties concerned to respond appropriately'.

2. Conflict is a reality in every human organisation. It can be positive when it presses us to confront difficult issues and disagreements that we might prefer to avoid. It can be creative. However, abuse against individuals or groups within the church is unacceptable.

Roman Catholic Church

A spokesperson for the Catholic Bishops' Conference of England and Wales maintains that they have good policies in their schools (this is, of course, required by law), but was confident there is no bullying in their churches.

Other Countries

Australia

In Australia each state has its own legislation; Australia probably has the most stringent laws and practices in order to prevent and deal with workplace bullying, wherever it occurs. However, only two states have a code of practice specifically for workplace bullying. WorkSafe Victoria has announced that employers have new duties to manage psychosocial hazards.[7] The Occupational Health and Safety (Psychological Health) Regulations 2025 came into effect on 1 December 2025. These regulations require employers to:

- identify and control psychosocial hazards and risks
- review and revise risk control measures for psychosocial hazards in certain circumstances.

The Uniting Church is the union of Methodist, Presbyterian and Congregational churches in Australia. The Synod of Victoria and Tasmania set up the Bethel Centre in 1997 to offer counselling and supervision to its members. It is, however, independent of the Synod. Bethel's services are available to individuals who have experienced trauma, abuse, or misuse of power emotionally, spiritually, physically or sexually within the Church:

> Abuse and misuse of power may include bullying, intimidation and harassment that can sometimes be found in congregations. Support is also offered to those accused of, or who identify as, being a perpetrator.[8]

It was originally set up because of the number of people known about who had suffered from bullying and harassment in the church. The coordinator and counsellors have wide experience of understanding bullying in any church community and are expert in knowing what resources are available through the Australian Human Rights Commission and WorkSafe Victoria. Bethel also points people to the relevant materials from both organisations on their website.

The Anglican Church of Australia has for many years been at the forefront of making sure that churches are safe places. The General Synod in 2022 passed the motion that it

> Deplores and condemns any behaviour that is disrespectful, hurtful, intentionally insensitive, bullying or abusive … (and) commits itself to fostering churches and fellowships where compassion and grace abound and where the love of God is expressed to all, so that our churches and ministries are welcoming, safe and respectful of all people.[9]

As a result of this the Anglican Communion Safe Church Commission produced 'Safe Church: How to start Guide' in 2023 https://www.anglicancommunion.org/resource/safe-church-how-to-start-guide-2/

Canada
Quebec (2004), Ontario (2010) and Saskatchewan (2007) have all made workplace bullying illegal.

Ireland
The Republic of Ireland has a code of practice for employers and employees on the prevention and resolution of bullying at work (2010).

Scandinavia
Sweden was the first country in the world with legislation in 1993. Denmark and Norway also have legislation making bullying illegal in workplaces.

United States

In the United States the first conference looking at workplace bullying was held in 2000. It was organised by what became the Workplace Bullying Institute, which has campaigned tirelessly for many years to get 'healthy workplace' bills into state and federal law. Since 2003 the Healthy Workplace Bill has been the basis of legislation in 32 states and two territories. A new bill, the Workplace Bullying Accountability Act, is currently being presented to large numbers of state legislatures.

There is no organisation which is looking specifically at bullying in churches.

The Workplace Bullying Institute conducted a US-wide survey in 2024 which found that 32 per cent of Americans (52.2 million) are bullied directly; 51 per cent of hybrid workers are targeted most; 55 per cent of bullying is top down, and 29 per cent is by peers. 87 per cent of the public support a new law to address bullying.

Bullying in Churches? Conclusions

Although the countries above have legislation specifically prohibiting bullying in the workplace, it would seem that only Australia and the UK have any understanding, information and help to deal specifically with bullying in churches. There is still considerable misunderstanding about the way to tackle bullying. The Methodist Church in the UK has taken a different route when trying to deal with bullying within their congregations and councils, by concentrating on working together positively. They have been generous enough to make their resources widely available to others. Too many dioceses in the Church of England and the national churches have not taken into account the considerable body of research looking at workplace bullying and have, therefore, not modified their policies and procedures in the light of their conclusions. A revised version of the Church of England report *Dignity at Work* which reflects this is urgently needed.

---

1. http://news.bbc.co.uk/1/hi/business/8439005.stm
2. https://www.churchofengland.org/resources/diocesan-resources/how-we-relate-one-another
3. https://www.methodist.org.uk/for-churches/guidance-for-churches/wellbeing/ ; https://www.methodist.org.uk/for-churches/guidance-for-churches/introducing-positive-working-together/ ; https://www.methodist.org.uk/for-churches/guidance-for-churches/introducing-positive-working-together/training-in-positive-working-together/ ; https://www.methodist.org.uk/for-churches/learning-and-development/learning-and-development-events/ .
4. https://www.baptist.org.uk/Articles/703824/BUGB_Guide_for.aspx
5. https://urc.org.uk/wp-content/uploads/2021/11/Good-Practice-5-Appendix-X-responding-to-allegations-of-bullying-and-harassment.pdf
6. https://www.worksafe.vic.gov.au/bullying
7. https://bethelcentre.com.au/our-services-copy-5/
8. https://anglican.org.au/the-general-synod/search-resolutions-of-gs-sessions/?sid=14184
9. https://www.anglicancommunion.org/media/507211/231120_SCC_Quick-Start-Guide-to-Implementing-Safe-Church-Practices_EN.pdf

23

What I've Learned from Bullies

JANET FIFE

I was 18 when I first met Larry. I'd been away to college, and when I returned home found the Vietnam veteran leading the youth group at the California church where my father had recently become pastor. The group consisted of people in their mid-teens to mid-twenties; Larry was 24. We met in his apartment, where the American flag that had draped his brother's coffin dominated one wall. The Jesus Movement was still underway, and we young people were keen. Larry led us in studies of A. W. Tozer's book *The Knowledge of the Holy,* on the attributes of God. The studies were good, and at their conclusion we often went out to Shakey's Pizza Parlour. It was a close-knit group.

Soon after I arrived Larry offered to 'counsel' me, but I didn't feel comfortable with that and declined. Larry in turn didn't seem happy with my refusal – which of course made me more wary as he continued to pressure me to confide in him. After a few months I became aware that Larry had 'counselled' every other member of the group, leading them to confess to him their secrets and failings. After some time I found out that Larry was holding these confessions over the young people in order to control them: if they didn't do as he said, he would tell their secrets. It was blackmail. He even blackmailed one attractive young woman into promising to marry him. The Sunday their engagement was announced, she was due to sing a solo. She looked dreadful, and with woebegone face announced she would sing, 'In times like these, we need a Saviour.' Hardly the picture of love's young dream.

Larry had other ways of keeping us under his thumb. He would make personal criticisms of us individually; anyone who displeased him was denounced as 'unspiritual'. In the heady atmosphere of a religious revival, that was a serious criticism. One evening I needed to use his bathroom: when I emerged I found he had gathered the whole group outside the door to listen while I used the facilities. It was excruciatingly embarrassing for a self-conscious teenager.

For some time I wrestled with the knowledge I had of the ways in which Larry was controlling the group, both collectively and individually. I didn't know what I ought to do. Eventually I told my father and one of the elders. I can't remember what action they took, but I remember the outcome: Larry left the church, along with every one of the young people. Larry ordered them not to come to church again, and not to speak to me. I was still fairly new in town, and in one fell swoop I lost every single one of my social group. It was an intensely lonely time. I knew that I had done the right thing in reporting Larry, but I was plagued with guilt for not having done it sooner. I felt that if I had, Larry might not have got such a grip on the young people that they all left with him. Looking back, with the benefit of 50 years' hindsight, I can see that it was probably already too late by the time I arrived on the scene. But the lesson I learned stayed with me: when you see something wrong, report it sooner rather than later.

There will always be people with a need to control others. The roots of that need will differ, as will the techniques they use. Some are subtle, some are blatant.

Some need to dominate whole communities or nations; others will target a small group or a few individuals. How vulnerable we are to those bullies will depend on a number of factors, including (but not exclusively) how much power the bully holds over us, the setting in which they operate, and whether they are lone wolves or operating in a pack. I once asked a wise priest/counsellor why I had so often been on the receiving end of bullying and sexual harassment. Was there something wrong with me? Was I doing something wrong? Andrew replied that he could see several factors which were not my fault: as one of the first women to be ordained in the Church of England, I was fair game for misogynists; I was single and had no immediate family in this country, so predators need not fear an angry husband or family members; and I had a background of abuse. People who have been abused in any way in childhood carry the scars into adulthood. Like carnivores picking out the sick animal in a herd, human predators sense the wounds we carry and instinctively know we will make easy prey.

Growing up in a violent and abusive home, and being physically small, I learned early to placate angry and aggressive people. This is known as the 'fawning response' to trauma; the urge to please others as a means of avoiding further harm. It was compounded by confused 'Christian' teaching encouraging meekness and self-sacrifice – an attitude I now summarise as 'Jesus wants you for a doormat'. In my case the learned fawning response and Christian teaching on submission were overlaid on a naturally feisty personality, a Fife family trait (we have a Trafalgar hero among our ancestors). I could go into battle on behalf of someone else, or on a matter of principle, but usually seemed unable to defend myself. For example, I would have been about 8 years old when we drove south from Chicago, where we then lived, to a holiday in Florida. Passing through Georgia, we stopped at a filling station which had four toilets: White Ladies, Coloured Women, White Gents, and Black Men. I was furious at this (then legal) racial discrimination, and promptly headed for the Coloured Women's toilet. I was physically prevented by my father, who said, 'The owner's got a shotgun!' I still wish I'd been able to defy both the racist owner and my father. Later, as an adult, I was walking the dog in isolated woods when I came across three boys about to throw a smaller boy off a low bridge. I ordered them to leave the boy alone – and they did. But faced with aggression aimed at me personally, I was paralysed.

I could face down a gang of teenagers about to throw a propane cylinder on a bonfire, but I wouldn't defend myself against unjust accusations. On one such occasion a colleague's wife ranted at me for several minutes, accusing me of treachery and gross disloyalty to her husband. I hadn't done what she accused me of, but I didn't deny it. Instead, seeing how upset she was, I hugged her. I now find it difficult to explain why I didn't say, 'It wasn't me', except that it was the fawning defence I'd learned as a child. Naturally, my attempt to comfort her only confirmed her suspicions of my guilt, and made a bad situation worse.

On another occasion a substantial bequest from a deceased parishioner coincided with a very good special offer on a new hymnbook. Our existing hymnbooks were limited and 25 years old; it seemed a good opportunity. We were assured by the deceased woman's family that she would have been delighted to see us spend the money in this way. As the church council discussed the matter, one man stood and shouted at me, 'You've fallen for the oldest trick in the book!' I might have said that after working in publishing and bookselling, I knew a good offer when I saw one – but I said nothing. I was learning not to fawn in response to aggression, but neither was I capable of asserting my own qualifications for making a sound decision. From that incident and similar situations I learned that failing to explain or defend yourself doesn't necessarily bring peace and harmony: it can promote misunderstanding and intensify conflict.

I used to be puzzled by New Testament examples of Jesus' followers standing up for themselves, in apparent contravention of his command to turn the other cheek. The Gospel writers show us Jesus himself often answering back to his accusers, including during his trial. It is only regarding the crucifixion, which he knows to be his Father's will, that he does not resist. In Acts 16 and 22 Paul asserts his rights as a Roman citizen; in Acts 23 he rebukes the high priest who has illegally ordered him to be hit in the mouth while giving evidence. He writes to his protégé Timothy, 'Let no one despise you because of your youth, but set the believers an example in speech and conduct, in love, in faith, in purity' (1 Tim. 4:12). Insisting on a certain amount of basic respect seems actually to be part of modelling good Christian conduct. I suspect Paul might equally have written, to others of his followers: 'Let no one despise you because of your sex or class or race ...' Let no one despise you.

How then are we to understand Jesus' admonition to 'turn the other cheek'? My spiritual director pointed me to a different way of understanding Matt 5:38-41 – a passage which Mahatma Gandhi cited as one of the inspirations for his policy of nonviolent resistance. Walter Wink, in his book *Engaging the Powers*,[1] discusses it in detail. In the example Jesus gives, it is the right cheek the assailant hits. He would have used his right hand, since the left, in first century Palestine as in twentieth-century India, was only used for unclean tasks. The only way in which you can strike someone's right cheek with your right hand is by using a backhanded slap. But backhanded slaps were a humiliating insult, by Jewish law to be inflicted only on one's inferiors. A heavy fine was imposed on those who administered a backhanded slap to an equal. Jesus advises those humiliated by a backhanded slap on the right cheek to turn their left cheek towards the assailant. If he hits you again it will have to be with the palm of his hand or his fist – and that will elevate you to the status of an equal. Far from being an instruction to let people walk all over you, turning the other cheek was a clever way of subverting the power of bullies and oppressors.

Going the extra mile turns the tables on persecutors in a similar way. Roman soldiers were allowed to make civilians carry their heavy packs for one Roman mile. Imagine how inconvenient, frustrating, and humiliating: whatever your status, no matter how important your own business, you would have to drop what you were doing and become a beast of burden for the occupying forces. But there was a limit: a soldier could not make you carry his pack for more than one mile. So, if instead of handing the pack over when you've walked one mile you keep carrying it, you take the initiative away from the soldier. In fact he now risks punishment. He would be much more cautious about treating the next person as a packhorse.

Jesus taught a way in which we could peacefully resist those who would subjugate us, while staying within the framework of law – and in fact using it to curb the power of bullies. It's a way, however, that requires courage and a certain amount of confidence. So while study of the Bible convinced me I need not be a doormat for Jesus, it was not on its own sufficient to cure my inability to stand up for myself. I needed psychotherapy to help undo the messages imbued in me in an abusive childhood –

messages that I had no worth in myself, but only in how I pleased others or what I achieved. I also needed people in my life who loved me consistently enough, even when I was unlovable, that I began to gain a sense of my own value. I was fortunate enough to find them, in the shape of close friends. As the Iona hymn puts it, the 'hands which shaped and saved the world/are present in the touch of friends.' It's very difficult to feel God's love unless you are loved by God's people. I have learned valuable lessons from bullies – but even more valuable lessons from those who have loved me.

---

[1] Wink, Walter, *Engaging the Powers: Discernment and Resistance in a World of Domination* (Minneapolis: Fortress Press, 1992), pp. 175-182.

Bibliography

Alison, J, *The Joy of Being Wrong: Original Sin Through Easter Eyes* (New York: Crossroad Publishing Company, 1998).

Avis, Paul, *Authority, Leadership and Conflict in the Church* (London: Mowbray, 1992).

Avis, Paul, *Shaping a Church of Ethical Integrity* (London: SCM, 2026).

Battin, Margaret P., *Ethics in the Sanctuary: Examining the Practices of Organized Religion* (Newhaven & London: Yale University Press, 1990).

Beasley-Murray, Paul, *Power for God's Sake: Power and abuse in the local church* (Eugene, OR: Wipf and Stock, 2005).

Benyei, C.R., *Understanding clergy misconduct in religious systems: Scapegoating, family secrets, and the abuse of power* (New York: Routledge, 1998).

Billenness, Clive, Is There a Psychopath in my Parish? https://www.youtube.com/ watch?v=UpJCgb5EY2s

Burgess, Neil, *Into Deep Water: The experience of curates in the Church of England* (Bury St. Edmunds: Kevin Mayhew, 1998).

Cherry, Stephen, *Healing Agony: Re-Imagining Forgiveness* (London: Continuum, 2012).

Coate, Mary Ann, *Clergy Stress: The hidden conflicts of ministry* (London: SPCK, 1989).

Du Mez, Kristin Kobes, *Jesus and John Wayne: How White Evangelicals Corrupted a Faith and Fractured a Nation* (New York: Liveright, 2020).

Dumitrescu, Irina, 'Are you a toxic enabler?' Times Higher Education, September 16, 2021.

Enroth, Ronald M., *Churches that Abuse* (Grand Rapids: Zondervan, 1992).

Field, Tim, *Bully in Sight: How to Predict, Resist, Challenge and Combat Workplace Bullying* (Wantage, Oxfordshire: Success Unlimited, 1996).

Fife, Janet, *To Be Honest* (London: DLT, 1993).

Fife, Janet, and Gilo, ed., *Letters to a Broken Church* (London: Ekklesia, 2019).

Finlan, Stephen, *Bullying in the Churches* (Eugene, OR: Cascade, 2015).

Forbes, Cheryl, *The Religion of Power* (Bromley: MarcEurope, 1983).

Ganzevoort, R. Ruard and Srdjan Sremac, eds., *Trauma and Lived Religion: Transcending the Ordinary* (Palgrave Studies in Lived Religion and Societal Challenges) (New York: Springer International Publishing AG, 2019).

Gardner, Fiona, *Night Sea Journeying: Soul Recovery from Childhood Trauma* (Eugene, OR: Cascade, 2025).

Gardner, Fiona, *Sex, Power, Control: Responding to Abuse in the Institutional Church* (Cambridge: Lutterworth Press, 2021).

Girard, Rene, *I See Satan Fall Like Lightning* (New York: Orbis, 2001).

Glasson, B., *A Spirituality of Survival* (London: Continuum, 2009).

Graystone, Andrew, *Bleeding for Jesus: John Smyth and the Cult of the Iwerne Camps: The Scandal that Shook the Church of England*, Revised edition (London: DLT, 2025).

Guiora, Amos N., *Armies of Enablers: Survivor Stories of Complicity and Betrayal in Sexual Assaults* (Chicago: ABA Publishing, 2020).

Harper, Rosie, and Alan Wilson, *To Heal and Not to Hurt: A fresh approach to safeguarding in the Church* (London: DLT, 2019).

Haugk, Kenneth C., *Antagonists in the Church: How to Identify and Deal with Destructive Conflict* (Minneapolis, MN: Augsburg Fortress, 1991).

Herman, J., ed., *Trauma and Recovery* (New York: Basic Books, 2015).

Howard, Roland, *The Rise and Fall of the Nine O'Clock Service: A cult within the Church?* (London: Mowbray, 1996).

Kruger, Michael J., *Bully Pulpit: Confronting the Problem of Spiritual Abuse in the Church* (Grand Rapids, MI: Zondervan Reflective, 2022).

Kushner, Harold S., *When Bad Things Happen to Good People* (New York: Anchor Books, 2004).

Langberg, Diane, *When the Church Harms God's People* (Grand Rapids, MI, Brazos Press: Baker Publishing Group, 2024).

Langberg, Diane, *Redeeming Power: Understanding Authority and Abuse in the Church* (Grand Rapids, MI, Brazos Press: Baker Publishing Group, 2020).

Leyens, J. Ph, M.P. Paladino, R.T. Rodriguez, J. Vaes, S. Demoulin, A.P. Rodriguez, and R. Gaunt, 'The emotional side of prejudice: The attribution of secondary emotions to ingroups and outgroups.' *Personality and Social Psychology Review* 4 (2): (2000).

Litchfield, Kate, *Tend my Flock: Sustaining Good Pastoral Care* (Norwich: Canterbury Press, 2006).

MacCulloch, Diarmaid, *Silence: A Christian History* (London: Penguin Books, 2014).

Martin, John, ed., *Curate's Egg: the inside story of what a curate's life is really like* (Crowborough: Highland Books, 1990).

Martin, Sheila, *A Guilty Secret: The bullying of ministers in the church* (Amazon: Kindle, 2013).

Maynard, Dennis, *When Sheep Attack* (Amazon: 2010).

Miller, Seumas, *The Moral Foundations of Social Institutions* (Cambridge: CUP, 2010).

Oakley, Lisa, and Justin Humphreys, *Escaping the Maze of Spiritual Abuse: Creating healthy Christian cultures* (London: SPCK, 2019).

Osborn, Lawrence & Andrew Walker, *Harmful Religion: An Exploration of Religious Abuse* (London: SPCK, 1997).

Parsons, Stephen, *Ungodly Fear: Fundamentalist Christianity and the Abuse of Power* (Oxford: Lion, 2000).

Pattison, S., *Shame, Theory, Therapy, Theology* (Cambridge: CUP, 2000).

Peck, M. Scott, *People of the Lie: The Hope for Healing Human Evil* (London: Arrow, 1990).

Rees, Christina (ed.), *Voices of this Calling: Experiences of the First Generation of Women Priests* (Norwich: Canterbury Press, 2002).

Rediger, G. Lloyd, *Clergy Killers: Guidance for Pastors and Congregations Under Attack* (Louisville, KY: Westminster/John Knox Press, 1997).

Ronson, John, *The Psychopath Test: a journey through the madness industry* (London: Picador, 2011).

Rossall, Judith, *Forbidden Fruit and Fig Leaves: Reading the Bible with the Shamed* (London: SCM, 2020).

Ross-McNairn, Jonathon, and Sonia Barron, *Being a Curate: Stories of what it's really like* (London: SPCK, 2014).

Sanford, John A., *Ministry Burnout* (Louisville, KY: Westminster/ John Knox Press, 1982).

Spurgeon, Charles, 'The Minister's Fainting Fits,' in *Lectures to My Students* (available in multiple editions, including on Kindle).

Stone, Selina, *A Heavy Yoke: Theology, Power and Abuse in the Church* (London: SCM, 2025).

Taylor, Barbara Brown, *God in Pain: Teaching Sermons on Suffering* (Nashville: Abingdon,1998).

Van der Kolk, Bessel A., *The Body Keeps the Score: Brain, Mind, Body, in the Healing of Trauma* (New York: Viking Penguin, 2014).

Van Knippenberg, Daan & Michael A. Hogg, eds, *Leadership and Power: Identity Processes in Groups and Organizations* (London: Sage Publications, 2003).

Van-Vonderen, J., *When God's People Let You Down* (Bloomington, MN: Bethany House, 1995).

Vos, Matthew S., *Strangers and Scapegoats: Extending God's Welcome to Those on the Margins* (Grand Rapids: Baker, 2022).

White, Sheila, *An Introduction to the Psychodynamics of Workplace Bullying* (London: Karnac, 2013).

Willams, Kipling, *Ostracism: The Power of Silence* (New York: Guilford Press, 2001)

Wink, Walter, *The Powers, Vol. 1: Naming the Powers: The Language of Power in the New Testament* (Philadelphia: Fortress Press, 1984).

Wink, Walter, *The Powers, Vol. 2: Unmasking the Powers: The Invisible Forces that Determine Human Existence* (Philadelphia: Fortress Press, 1986).

Wink, Walter, *The Powers, Vol. 3: Engaging the Powers: Discernment and Resistance in a World of Domination* (Philadelphia: Fortress Press, 1992).

Websites for resources:

Balmnet (Bullied and Abused Lives in Ministry), https://www.balmnet.co.uk

Bridge Builders, https://www.bbministries.org.uk

StopBullying.Gov (US Department of Health and Human Services).

Surviving Church, blogs on power and abuse of power, ed. Stephen Parsons, https://survivingchurch.org

The Sheldon Hub: doing healthy ministry together, https://www.sheldonhub.org